Attack of the B Queens

NO MAN CAN TOUCH HER NAKED STEEL
Boris ©85
BARBARIAN QUEEN
Starring LANA CLARKSON · KATT SHEA · FRANK ZAGARINO · DAWN DUNLAP
Produced by FRANK ISAAC and ALEX SESSA Screenplay by HOWARD R. COHEN
Directed by HECTOR OLIVERA

Attack of the B Queens

edited by Jon Keeyes

Luminary Press
Baltimore, Maryland

ISBN 1-887664-08-4
Library of Congress Catalog Card Number 2003111721
Manufactured in the United States of America
Printed by King Printing, Lowell, MA
First Printing by Luminary Press: an imprint of Midnight Marquee Press, Inc.,
September 2003

To my Aunt Wendie.
Thanks for the wonderful years of
Halloween horror.

Table of Contents

AND THE KING SPEAKS:
An Introduction
by Roger Corman

Welcome to the world of B film actresses, and join me on a fascinating tour through their lives and films.

As you delve into this book, you'll see that B film actresses are not only good to look at, but also bring a dimension of psychological and sexual challenge, humanity and wit to the more straightforward pleasures of the action-based B movie.

The category of B film actress is essentially a fluid one. The main-

stream film business has always drawn on new talent making their debuts in B film: for example, in movies I've produced, the actresses I've introduced include Sandra Bullock, Sherilynn Fenn, Talia Shire and Pam Grier. Also, adventurous established actresses from time to time choose to appear in a B movie because it features a strong female role in a controversial story of a kind that the major studios stay away from. Some of the remarkable actresses to whom I am personally grateful for undertaking challenging roles in movies I have produced or directed include Angie Dickinson, Sally Kirkland, Diane Ladd and Shelley Winters.

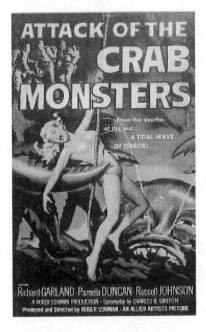

B film actresses also frequently acquire their own cult following and inspire great loyalty from their fans. Simply look to some of my recently produced films and you will find favorite B film leading ladies like Lisa Boyle, Lana Clarkson, Maria Ford and Julie Strain.

As a director, my films have benefited from the intelligence as well as the talent and good looks of many of these principal actresses. When I was starting out as a director, the quick-witted Beverly Garland, one of my favorite actresses, saved me from making a crucial mistake. I was quite proud of the fact that I had designed the monster for my science fiction movie, *It Conquered the World*, on scientific principles: since the monster came from Venus, a planet with heavy gravity, it would, I reasoned, have to be low to the ground and very massive. So it was built low and squat. In between takes, Beverly strolled up to the monster and looked down at it, sneering. "So you've come to conquer the world, huh?" She gave a ferocious laugh. Then she reared back and kicked it. That was how she taught me that I might be right scientifically, but wrong dramatically. The monster must always be bigger than the leading lady.

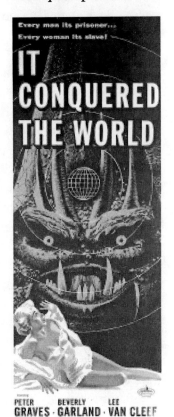

I owe a considerable part of my success as a filmmaker to the contributions of the talented actresses who have worked with me, and in conclusion I thank them all warmly, as I invite you to explore the world of B film actresses and celebrate their past and continuing contributions to the movies.

THE BIRTH OF THE B:
The Silent Era
through the 1950s
by Jon Keeyes

In 1933 Fay Wray unleashed a scream that would seal her fate as the mother of all Scream Queens, and more appropriately, she would become known as the Grand Matriarch of horror film actresses. The film, of course, was *King Kong* (1933) and generations of horror film actresses would be compared to Fay's literal epitome of horror film scream queen: a beautiful, scantily clad female, who screams for dear life. While actresses have gained fame and fortune playing a wide range of characters—from vulnerable vixens, to cast-iron bitches, to the rough and tough heroines—it is Fay Wray who will be immortalized in the annals of horror film history as its grand dame.

Although technically scream queens grew to prominence with Fay Wray and the movies of her era, the term "scream queen" or "B Queen" had not yet been conceived.

Unfortunately, when people hear the term "B film," images of low-budget 1950s sci-fi movies, which feature bad monster suits and well-endowed, screaming damsels in distress, who are forced to spout ridiculous dialogue, come to mind. Actually, this image is partly correct, for the quickie horror and science fiction flicks of the early 20th century helped create the popular conception of what today is considered a B film, although the theories and Hollywood history of B films have become so confused and overthought that it's difficult to state with any certainty the evolution of the term.

One theory is that the term B film came about primarily as a result of movie houses and drive-in theaters that featured double bills during the 1940s; the first feature was the "A" film and the secondary feature was the "B" film. Initially, these B films were not necessarily independent productions. In fact, the first B films produced came directly from studios such as Universal and RKO. These B films tended to be lower-budgeted movies than the A films and were quickly shot, featuring as

Fay Wray found not only a giant ape, but also stardom: 1933's *King Kong*.

many gimmicks and as much cleavage as possible—hopefully to attract masses of teenagers eager to spend their money on a little titillation and a lot of screams.

Today B films have taken on a whole new meaning. Like Frankenstein seeking to reanimate the dead, the defining nature of B films has been newly recreated almost every decade. From the 1940s through the 1970s, B films tended to focus on horror, science fiction, crime and West-

Only one thing kept her alive.

WHITE SLAVE

BASED ON A TRUE STORY

ern topics and were created by second units at the studios. Or, they were independently produced exploitation movies that sought to provide as much sex and nudity as possible surrounded by a shell that was laughingly referred to as a script. These films played drive-ins, specialty theaters and art houses and occasionally found their way to feature theaters.

In the 1980s, the term B film was again redefined—pop culture termed direct-to-video movies B films—regardless of genre, content or quality. Would-be filmmakers were able to throw together thousands of films for little money and sell them direct-to-video for a quickie profit. These films were churned out for a fraction of the cost of a theatrical film. These guerrilla filmmakers were also able to bypass the censorship of the Motion Picture Association's rating board—they could show as much naked flesh and streaming blood as they liked. If any decade in film history can be identified with today's pop culture definition for B film, it was the 1980s.

As the '80s came to a close, B films were given new life once again with the mass availability of cable television and the growing popularity of erotic features (such as those produced by *Playboy* and *Penthouse*). Blood and guts ran amok in the 1980s and science fiction was overshadowed by television shows such as *Star Trek: The Next Generation* and *Babylon 5*, and the male-dominated audience wanted a change. As fast as they could grope them, production companies snatched up Playmates and Pets to star in their erotic horror/suspense films, thereby drawing on as much repressed sexual lust as possible. B films became low-budget product shot directly for cable, competing with the direct-to-video market.

By the close of the 20th century, the term B film would become a catch-all phrase—an all-encompassing term for horror, science fiction and erotic films; ergo anything low-budget. The big budget of an A production in the 1930s would barely film a commercial today. Films considered classics in the 1950s today appear campy and laughable compared to modern computer-enhanced, special effects-riddled films. So, B films have become a catchall based upon the perception and definition of the current generation of movie fans. With the exception of film critics and historians, B films will always be identified with the horror, science fiction and erotic genres and their loyal fan following.

What then does this have to do with actresses and the birth of B films? In order to discuss the actresses we first have to define the films they are related to. Actresses such as Brinke Stevens, Linnea Quigley and Michelle Bauer may forever be known as the legendary Scream Queens, but their roles, and the styles of films they appeared in, had to be born from some mad filmmaker's dream. It is from the beginning of film through the 1950s that the seeds of the modern B film genre were planted.

The first five or so decades of cinema were filled with now-forgotten films, which sought to attract audiences eager for the forbidden and the naughty, a theme popularized by studios like Universal. The 1920s un-

***The Cabinet of Dr. Caligari* would influence future filmmakers.**

leashed bizarre sex and horror films to eager crowds, but this would change with the advent of the all-powerful Hays commission.

The audiences of the past have much in common with the modern film audience: men want to see women with as few clothes as possible—boys want frightening films, which coerce their dates to cling to their arm—and women want strong heroines they can empathize with. From the suffragist movement to suburban moms and women trying to break the glass ceiling, female audiences enjoy seeing laser gun-wielding, butt-kicking heroines as much as the guys. Not that all female roles in the early history of film were strong—they were more often than not damsels in distress—but there was a greater chance of feisty heroines in the realm of genre flicks.

The genre of modern B films can be traced all the way back to the silent film era, beginning with a series of influential movies: *Alraune* (1918), *The Cabinet of Dr. Caligari* (1919), *Nosferatu* (1922) and *Metropolis* (1926). While these were not considered low-budget or B films by anyone in their right mind, these films would directly influence fu-

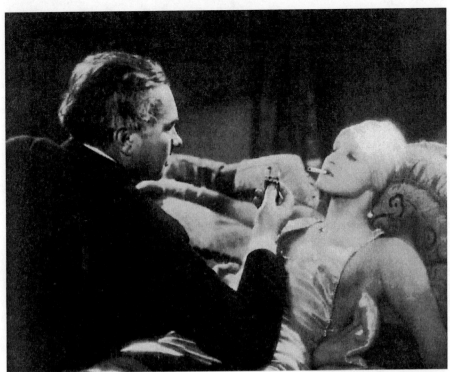

Brigitte Helm and Paul Wegener in the 1928 *Alraune*

ture filmmakers in their enduring struggle to create a grand film with little money as well as influencing filmmakers' creations of horror, science fiction and erotic movies for years to come. These films would become the example of how to film with style and using techniques that relied upon camera angles, emotions and the ability to create a set from nothing. They also featured the main attraction of any good B film: beautiful women.

Two separate versions of *Alraune* appeared in 1918. The first came from director Eugen Illes, in which Hilde Worter portrayed a prostitute kidnapped by a mad scientist and artificially inseminated with the semen from a hanged murderer. The second was from Mihaly Kertesz (later known as Michael Curtiz) in which his prostitute (played by Gyula Gál) is forced to mate with a mandrake root growing below the hanged murderer. In both cases, the scientist produces a soulless woman who inevitably turns on him. Unfortunately, it appears that both versions are now lost. However, the title does reemerge when Brigitte Helm plays the bitter woman in a silent film version (1928), which was followed two years later by a sound version.

Jane (Lil Dagover) is kidnapped by Cesare (Conrad Veidt) in *The Cabinet of Dr. Caligari*.

Considered the first international horror feature, *The Cabinet of Dr. Caligari* was made for 18,000 marks and introduced psychological horror with a twist ending. In a small German village, a circus sideshow hypnotist introduces his somnambulist, a perpetually sleeping man who is commanded by the voice of the doctor. Residing in a coffin, the somnambulist's gaunt face and eerie home brought terror to many a young girl's heart. Eventually in the town a series of murders begins as the film steadily weaves its horrific tale of control and deceit.

For *The Cabinet of Dr. Caligari*, director Robert Wiene recruited a dark-haired beauty with haunting eyes named Lil Dagover. Lil had made her way into German cinema via her marriage to established actor Fritz Daghofer. Though she had already appeared in a few films, her role in *The Cabinet of Dr. Caligari* as the fragile heroine named Jane would jump-start her career. Lil's accomplishments would explode from this point, eventually earning her the West German Cross of Merit in 1967. Though her glory days would end in the late 1930s, Lil continued to

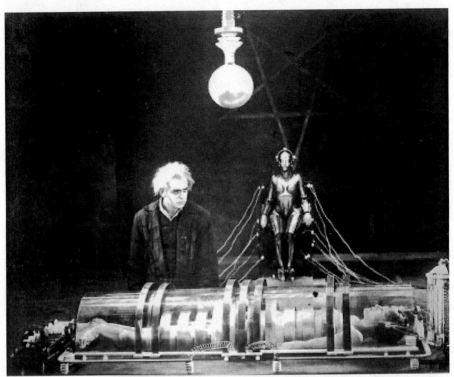

***Metropolis* can never be considered a B film.**

appear in films until the time of her death in 1980. Her career spanned 65 years and 118 movies.

Nosferatu (originally released in Germany as *Nosferatu, eine Symphonie des Grauens*) expanded the horror theme by focusing on the eternally seductive vampire. The vampire is perhaps the most alluring creature in film history—the vampire "kiss" being the most tasteful yet erotic convention to ever be introduced to cinema. Though Max Schreck's rendition of the vampire is hideous and ugly, it is his female co-star who creates the eroticism.

Played by Greta Schroeder, this charming actress would capture the essence of the B film heroine with exaggerated gestures, boldly overstated fearful eyes and sustained screams—well, yes, it was silent film but such exaggerated actions would become the staple of every good latter-day B queen. What's a good B film without an actress using overly dramatic gestures?

As for *Metropolis*, this hugely expansive science fiction movie was over a year in production and cost millions—a long way from a B film.

But science fiction films are one of the three key themes in the modern B film genre and *Metropolis* became a model by which all future sci-fi would be crafted. The standard treatment of sci-fi women would begin with *Metropolis'* female characters, who wore skimpy, futuristic clothing and appeared seductively feminine. However, the women were depicted as equals or near-to-equal with their male counterparts. This may sound awfully chauvinistic but the perception of the era has to be taken into consideration.

In the early days of film, typical female roles were as frightened victims, seductive villainesses or scatter-brained comedians. It would not be until the late 1950s and early '60s that female characters would begin to gain equality [see page 173, "Queen Bitches of the Universe" for the notable exceptions].

Set in the year 2026, *Metropolis* focuses upon an enslaved society forced to live below ground while the upper class live in luxury surrounded by gigantic skyscrapers. The female lead is played by Brigitte Helm who plays Maria, a selfless woman seeking to unite the downtrodden workers, and an evil android designed identical in appearance to Maria. David Thomson in *Omni's Screen Flights, Screen Fantasies* remarks:

> Whereas Maria is innocent and altruistic, the robot-temptress explodes on screen in a lascivious, near-naked dance that is among the most erotic sequences in silent film.

It is this erotic nature that would catapult future B queens to eternal fame and garner them a devoted fan following of hormone-driven teenage boys and ambitious adult purveyors of beauty and sexuality.

Horror and sexually suggestive material became an increasing staple of the early B genre. Just as the 1980s saw family activists protesting the non-rated, highly explicit, direct-to-video films, early filmmakers experienced the same mouth-foaming frenzy. In 1922, the Motion Picture Producers and Distributors of America was established and quickly became the maverick filmmakers' worst nightmare. The official press release from the MPAA notes:

> The MPAA was formed by major Hollywood companies in 1922 as the Motion Picture Producers and Distributors Association. Even with the name change to the Motion Picture Association of America, the main activity of the Association has been political, and the companies have always hired well-connected Washington insiders to represent their interests in the capital.
> The first head was President Warren G. Harding's brilliant campaign manager, Will H. Hays. In his day Hays

became famous for the MPPDA production code, a set of moralistic restrictions governing the content of motion pictures. Hays retired in 1945.

Swimming star Annette Kellermann swam nude in *Neptune's Daughter* in 1914, this would never have been permitted by the censors after 1930.

The association was formed when the movie moguls recognized the impact religious organizations and morally minded action groups could have on profits. But like all safeguards, resourceful filmmakers found ways around the censors. Although the association was formed in 1922, Hays wouldn't begin to really impact the content of films until 1930 with the advent of the production code. The 1920s, an era of bootleggers, bobs and flappers, were filled with titillating films that shocked many and bared all. These risqué films were marketed toward specialty theaters and traveling road shows, and were often slyly labeled educational films. Unfortunately, most of these films have been lost forever.

In his *The Incredibly Strange Film Book*, Jonathan Ross noted that filmmakers of this era became professors, who used sex, drugs and violence to "educate" audiences on the darker side of life. Usually erotic and exciting, this educational approach to morally indecent subject matter allowed filmmakers to get around the new morality. Authors Felicia Feaster and Bret Wood devoted an entire book, *Forbidden Fruit: The Golden Age of the Exploitation Film* (Midnight Marquee Press, Inc., 1999) to this very subject.

Avid readers of genre history have constantly seen references to the infamous Hays Code. But how many readers have actually seen the offending document? So, in the interests of film history—or for readers' amusement, we hereby give you the MPPC.

The Motion Picture Production Code of 1930 (Hays Code)

If motion pictures present stories that will affect lives for the better, they can become the most powerful force for the improvement of mankind

A Code to Govern the Making of Talking, Synchronized and Silent Motion Pictures. Formulated and formally adopted by The Association of Motion Picture Producers, Inc. and The Motion Picture Producers and Distributors of America, Inc. in March 1930.

Motion picture producers recognize the high trust and confidence which have been placed in them by the people of the world and which have made motion pictures a universal form of entertainment.

They recognize their responsibility to the public because of this trust and because entertainment and art are important influences in the life of a nation.

Hence, though regarding motion pictures primarily as entertainment without any explicit purpose of teaching or propaganda, they know that the motion picture within its own field of entertainment may be directly responsible for spiritual or moral progress, for higher types of social life, and for much correct thinking.

During the rapid transition from silent to talking pictures they have realized the necessity and the opportunity of subscribing to a Code to govern the production of talking pictures and of re-acknowledging this responsibility.

On their part, they ask from the public and from public leaders a sympathetic understanding of their purposes and problems and a spirit of cooperation that will allow them the freedom and opportunity necessary to bring the motion picture to a still higher level of wholesome entertainment for all the people.

General Principles

1. No picture shall be produced that will lower the moral standards of those who see it. Hence the sympathy of the audience should never be thrown to the side of crime, wrongdoing, evil or sin.

2. Correct standards of life, subject only to the requirements of drama and entertainment, shall be presented.

3. Law, natural or human, shall not be ridiculed, nor shall sympathy be created for its violation.

Particular Applications

I. Crimes Against the Law
These shall never be presented in such a way as to throw sympathy with the crime as against law and justice or to inspire others with a desire for imitation.

1. Murder

   a. The technique of murder must be presented in a way that will not inspire imitation.

   b. Brutal killings are not to be presented in detail.

   c. Revenge in modern times shall not be justified.

2. Methods of Crime should not be explicitly presented.

   a. Theft, robbery, safe-cracking, and dynamiting of trains, mines, buildings, etc., should not be detailed in method.

   b. Arson must subject to the same safeguards.

   c. The use of firearms should be restricted to the essentials.

   d. Methods of smuggling should not be presented.

3. Illegal drug traffic must never be presented.

4. The use of liquor in American life, when not required by the plot or for proper characterization, will not be shown.

II. Sex
The sanctity of the institution of marriage and the home shall be upheld. Pictures shall not infer that low forms of sex relationship are the accepted or common thing.

1. Adultery, sometimes necessary plot material, must not be explicitly treated, or justified, or presented attractively.

2. Scenes of Passion

   a. They should not be introduced when not essential to the plot.

b. Excessive and lustful kissing, lustful embraces, suggestive postures and gestures, are not to be shown.

c. In general passion should so be treated that these scenes do not stimulate the lower and baser element.

3. Seduction or Rape

a. They should never be more than suggested, and only when essential for the plot, and even then never shown by explicit method.

b. They are never the proper subject for comedy.

4. Sex perversion or any inference to it is forbidden.

5. White slavery shall not be treated.

6. Miscegenation (sex relationships between the white and black races) is forbidden.

7. Sex hygiene and venereal diseases are not subjects for motion pictures.

8. Scenes of actual child birth, in fact or in silhouette, are never to be presented.

9. Children's sex organs are never to be exposed.

III. Vulgarity
The treatment of low, disgusting, unpleasant, though not necessarily evil, subjects should always be subject to the dictates of good taste and a regard for the sensibilities of the audience.

IV. Obscenity
Obscenity in word, gesture, reference, song, joke, or by suggestion (even when likely to be understood only by part of the audience) is forbidden.

V. Profanity
Pointed profanity (this includes the words, God, Lord, Jesus, Christ - unless used reverently - Hell, S.O.B., damn, Gawd), or every other profane or vulgar expression however used, is forbidden.

VI. Costume
1. Complete nudity is never permitted. This includes nudity in fact or in silhouette, or any lecherous or licentious notice thereof by other characters in the picture.

2. Undressing scenes should be avoided, and never used save where essential to the plot.

3. Indecent or undue exposure is forbidden.

4. Dancing or costumes intended to permit undue exposure or indecent movements in the dance are forbidden.

VII. Dances
1. Dances suggesting or representing sexual actions or indecent passions are forbidden.

2. Dances which emphasize indecent movements are to be regarded as obscene.

VIII. Religion
1. No film or episode may throw ridicule on any religious faith.

2. Ministers of religion in their character as ministers of religion should not be used as comic characters or as villains.

3. Ceremonies of any definite religion should be carefully and respectfully handled.

IX. Locations
The treatment of bedrooms must be governed by good taste and delicacy.

X. National Feelings
1. The use of the Flag shall be consistently respectful.

2. The history, institutions, prominent people and citizenry of other nations shall be represented fairly.

XI. Titles
Salacious, indecent, or obscene titles shall not be used.

XII. Repellent Subjects

The following subjects must be treated within the careful limits of good taste:
1. Actual hangings or electrocutions as legal punishments for crime.
2. Third degree methods.
3. Brutality and possible gruesomeness.
4. Branding of people or animals.
5. Apparent cruelty to children or animals.
6. The sale of women, or a woman selling her virtue.
7. Surgical operations.

Reasons Supporting the Preamble of the Code

I. Theatrical motion pictures, that is, pictures intended for the theatre as distinct from pictures intended for churches, schools, lecture halls, educational movements, social reform movements, etc., are primarily to be regarded as ENTERTAINMENT.

Mankind has always recognized the importance of entertainment and its value in rebuilding the bodies and souls of human beings.

But it has always recognized that entertainment can be a character either HELPFUL or HARMFUL to the human race, and in consequence has clearly distinguished between:

a. Entertainment which tends to improve the race, or at least to re-create and rebuild human beings exhausted with the realities of life; and

b. Entertainment which tends to degrade human beings, or to lower their standards of life and living.

Hence the MORAL IMPORTANCE of entertainment is something which has been universally recognized. It enters intimately into the lives of men and women and affects them closely; it occupies their minds and affections during leisure hours; and ultimately touches the whole of their lives. A man may be judged by his standard of entertainment as easily as by the standard of his work.

So correct entertainment raises the whole standard of a nation.

Wrong entertainment lowers the whole living conditions and moral ideals of a race.

Note, for example, the healthy reactions to healthful sports, like baseball, golf; the unhealthy reactions to sports like cockfighting, bullfighting, bear baiting, etc.

Note, too, the effect on ancient nations of gladiatorial combats, the obscene plays of Roman times, etc.

II. Motion pictures are very important as ART.

Though a new art, possibly a combination art, it has the same object as the other arts, the presentation of human thought, emotion, and experience, in terms of an appeal to the soul through the senses.

Here, as in entertainment, Art enters intimately into the lives of human beings. Art can be morally good, lifting men to higher levels. This has been done through good music, great painting, authentic fiction, poetry, drama.

Art can be morally evil it its effects. This is the case clearly enough with unclean art, indecent books, suggestive drama. The effect on the lives of men and women are obvious.

Note: It has often been argued that art itself is unmoral, neither good nor bad. This is true of the THING which is music, painting, poetry, etc. But the THING is the PRODUCT of some person's mind, and the intention of that mind was either good or bad morally when it produced the thing. Besides, the thing has its EFFECT upon those who come into contact with it. In both these ways, that is, as a product of a mind and as the cause of definite effects, it has a deep moral significance and unmistakable moral quality.

Hence: The motion pictures, which are the most popular of modern arts for the masses, have their moral quality from the intention of the minds which produce them and from their effects on the moral lives and reactions of their audiences. This gives them a most important morality.

1. They reproduce the morality of the men who use the pictures as a medium for the expression of their ideas and ideals.

2. They affect the moral standards of those who, through the screen, take in these ideas and ideals.

In the case of motion pictures, the effect may be particularly emphasized because no art has so quick and so widespread an appeal to the masses. It has become in an incredibly short period the art of the multitudes.

III. The motion picture, because of its importance as entertainment and because of the trust placed in it by the peoples of the world, has special MORAL OBLIGATIONS:

A. Most arts appeal to the mature. This art appeals at once to every class, mature, immature, developed, undeveloped, law abiding, criminal. Music has its grades for different classes; so has literature and drama. This art of the motion picture, combining as it does the two fundamental appeals of looking at a picture and listening to a story, at once reaches every class of society.

B. By reason of the mobility of film and the ease of picture distribution, and because the possibility of duplicating positives in large quantities, this art reaches places unpenetrated by other forms of art.

C. Because of these two facts, it is difficult to produce films intended for only certain classes of people. The exhibitors' theatres are built for the masses, for the cultivated and the rude, the mature and the immature, the self-respecting and the criminal. Films, unlike books and music, can with difficulty be confined to certain selected groups.

D. The latitude given to film material cannot, in consequence, be as wide as the latitude given to book material. In addition:

a. A book describes; a film vividly presents. One presents on a cold page; the other by apparently living people.

b. A book reaches the mind through words merely; a film reaches the eyes and ears through the reproduction of actual events.

c. The reaction of a reader to a book depends largely on the keenness of the reader's imagination; the reaction to a film depends on the vividness of presentation.

Hence many things which might be described or suggested in a book could not possibly be presented in a film.

E. This is also true when comparing the film with the newspaper.

a. Newspapers present by description, films by actual presentation.

b. Newspapers are after the fact and present things as having taken place; the film gives the events in the process of enactment and with apparent reality of life.

F. Everything possible in a play is not possible in a film:

a. Because of the larger audience of the film, and its consequential mixed character. Psychologically, the larger the audience, the lower the moral mass resistance to suggestion.

b. Because through light, enlargement of character, presentation, scenic emphasis, etc., the screen story is brought closer to the audience than the play.

c. The enthusiasm for and interest in the film actors and actresses, developed beyond anything of the sort in history, makes the audience largely sympathetic toward the characters they portray and the stories in which they figure. Hence the audience is more ready to confuse actor and actress and the characters they portray, and it is most receptive of the emotions and ideals presented by the favorite stars.

G. Small communities, remote from sophistication and from the hardening process which often takes place in the ethical and moral standards of larger cities, are easily and readily reached by any sort of film.

H. The grandeur of mass settings, large action, spectacular features, etc., affects and arouses more intensely the emotional side of the audience.

In general, the mobility, popularity, accessibility, emotional appeal, vividness, straightforward presentation of fact in the film make for more intimate contact with a larger audience and for greater emotional appeal.

Hence the larger moral responsibilities of the motion pictures.

Reasons Underlying the General Principles

I. No picture shall be produced which will lower the moral standards of those who see it. Hence the sympathy of the audience should never be thrown to the side of crime, wrong-doing, evil or sin.

This is done:

1. When evil is made to appear attractive and alluring, and good is made to appear unattractive.

2. When the sympathy of the audience is thrown on the side of crime, wrongdoing, evil, sin. The same is true of a film that would throw sympathy against goodness, honor, innocence, purity or honesty.

Note: Sympathy with a person who sins is not the same as sympathy with the sin or crime of which he is guilty. We may feel sorry for the plight of the murderer or even understand the circumstances which led him to his crime: we may not feel sympathy with the wrong which he has done. The presentation of evil is often essential for art or fiction or drama. This in itself is not wrong provided:

a. That evil is not presented alluringly. Even if later in the film the evil is condemned or punished, it must not be allowed to appear so attractive that the audience's emotions are drawn to desire or approve so strongly that later the condemnation is forgotten and only the apparent joy of sin is remembered.

b. That throughout, the audience feels sure that evil is wrong and good is right.

II. Correct standards of life shall, as far as possible, be presented.

A wide knowledge of life and of living is made possible through the film. When right standards are consistently presented, the motion picture exercises the most powerful influences. It builds character, develops right ideals, inculcates correct principles, and all this in attractive story form.

If motion pictures consistently hold up for admiration high types of characters and present stories that will affect lives for the better, they can become the most powerful force for the improvement of mankind.

III. Law, natural or human, shall not be ridiculed, nor shall sympathy be created for its violation.

By natural law is understood the law which is written in the hearts of all mankind, the greater underlying principles of right and justice dictated by conscience.

By human law is understood the law written by civilized nations.

1. The presentation of crimes against the law is often necessary for the carrying out of the plot. But the presentation must not throw sympathy with the crime as against the law nor with the criminal as against those who punish him.

2. The courts of the land should not be presented as unjust. This does not mean that a single court may not be presented as unjust, much less that a single court official must not be presented this way. But the court system of the country must not suffer as a result of this presentation.

Reasons Underlying the Particular Applications

I. Sin and evil enter into the story of human beings and hence in themselves are valid dramatic material.

II. In the use of this material, it must be distinguished between sin which repels by its very nature, and sins which often attract.

a. In the first class come murder, most theft, many legal crimes, lying, hypocrisy, cruelty, etc.

b. In the second class come sex sins, sins and crimes of apparent heroism, such as banditry, daring thefts, leadership in evil, organized crime, revenge, etc.

The first class needs less care in treatment, as sins and crimes of this class are naturally unattractive. The audience instinctively condemns all such and is repelled.

Hence the important objective must be to avoid the hardening of the audience, especially of those who are young and impressionable, to the thought and fact of crime. People can become accustomed even to murder, cruelty, brutality, and repellent crimes, if these are too frequently repeated.

The second class needs great care in handling, as the response of human nature to their appeal is obvious. This is treated more fully below.

III. A careful distinction can be made between films intended for general distribution, and films intended for use in theatres restricted to a limited audience.

Themes and plots quite appropriate for the latter would be altogether out of place and dangerous in the former.

Note: The practice of using a general theatre and limiting its patronage to "Adults Only" is not completely satisfactory and is only partially effective.

However, maturer minds may easily understand and accept without harm subject matter in plots which do younger people positive harm.

Hence: If there should be created a special type of theatre, catering exclusively to an adult audience, for plays of this character (plays with problem themes, difficult discussions and maturer treatment) it would seem to afford an outlet, which does not now exist, for pictures unsuitable for general distribution but permissible for exhibitions to a restricted audience.

I. Crimes Against the Law
The treatment of crimes against the law must not:

1. Teach methods of crime.
2. Inspire potential criminals with a desire for imitation.
3. Make criminals seem heroic and justified.

Revenge in modern times shall not be justified. In lands and ages of less developed civilization and moral principles, revenge may sometimes be presented. This would be the case especially in places where no law exists to cover the crime because of which revenge is committed.

Because of its evil consequences, the drug traffic should not be presented in any form. The existence of the trade should not be brought to the attention of audiences.

The use of liquor should never be excessively presented. In scenes from American life, the necessities of plot and proper characterization alone justify its use. And in this case, it should be shown with moderation.

II. Sex
Out of a regard for the sanctity of marriage and the home, the triangle, that is, the love of a third party for one already married, needs careful handling. The treatment should not throw sympathy against marriage as an institution.

Scenes of passion must be treated with an honest acknowledgment of human nature and its normal reactions. Many scenes cannot be presented without arousing dangerous emotions on the part of the immature, the young or the criminal classes.

Even within the limits of pure love, certain facts have been universally regarded by lawmakers as outside the limits of safe presentation.

Attack of the B Queens

In the case of impure love, the love which society has always regarded as wrong and which has been banned by divine law, the following are important:

1. Impure love must not be presented as attractive and beautiful.

2. It must not be the subject of comedy or farce, or treated as material for laughter.

3. It must not be presented in such a way to arouse passion or morbid curiosity on the part of the audience.

4. It must not be made to seem right and permissible.

5. It general, it must not be detailed in method and manner.

III. Vulgarity; IV. Obscenity; V. Profanity; hardly need further explanation than is contained in the Code.

VI. Costume
General Principles:

1. The effect of nudity or semi-nudity upon the normal man or woman, and much more upon the young and upon immature persons, has been honestly recognized by all lawmakers and moralists.

2. Hence the fact that the nude or semi-nude body may be beautiful does not make its use in the films moral. For, in addition to its beauty, the effect of the nude or semi-nude body on the normal individual must be taken into consideration.

3. Nudity or semi-nudity used simply to put a "punch" into a picture comes under the head of immoral actions. It is immoral in its effect on the average audience.

4. Nudity can never be permitted as being necessary for the plot. Semi-nudity must not result in undue or indecent exposures.

5. Transparent or translucent materials and silhouette are frequently more suggestive than actual exposure.

VII. Dances
Dancing in general is recognized as an art and as a beautiful form of expressing human emotions.

But dances which suggest or represent sexual actions, whether performed solo or with two or more; dances intended to excite the emotional reaction of an audience; dances with movement of the breasts, excessive body movements while the feet are stationary, violate decency and are wrong.

VIII. Religion
The reason why ministers of religion may not be comic characters or villains is simply because the attitude taken toward them may easily become the attitude taken toward religion in general. Religion is lowered in the minds of the audience because of the lowering of the audience's respect for a minister.

IX. Locations
Certain places are so closely and thoroughly associated with sexual life or with sexual sin that their use must be carefully limited.

X. National Feelings
The just rights, history, and feelings of any nation are entitled to most careful consideration and respectful treatment.

XI. Titles
As the title of a picture is the brand on that particular type of goods, it must conform to the ethical practices of all such honest business.

XII. Repellent Subjects
Such subjects are occasionally necessary for the plot. Their treatment must never offend good taste nor injure the sensibilities of an audience.

In essence, the Hays Code shut down studios that sought national feature distribution with sex- and violence-filled movies. It is here, during the period of 1922 through the creation of the Hays Code, that moviemakers can trace the foundations of today's definition of B films. Independent outfits began popping up and producing quickie films for these specific markets. Their films were shown around the country in small theaters (one at a time), rented halls and sometimes even tents. Ambitious filmmakers were eager to profit on audiences' forbidden desire for sex and horror on the silver screen.

While many of the early filmmakers were independent producers, there were some small studios which sought to stay on the national circuit, and thus was built Poverty Row. Poverty Row studios such as Chesterfield, Monogram, Majestic and Reliable became the first real low-budget outfits, usually renting space from the larger studios and filming at breakneck speed. These masters of bargain-basement filmmaking would avoid retakes and expensive actors, and would work with small crews. The editing process was fast and furious. More often than not, the films were riddled with continuity mistakes and poorly constructed

scenes, which only added to the charm of their campy nature. The Poverty Row studios and roadshow-traveling producers helped create the B film legacy.

The 1920s and 1930s saw a plethora of genre films make their way across the country. The Chesterfield Motion Picture Company alone produced more than a dozen films a year from 1925 through 1937. Like most of the low-budget companies of the era, Chesterfield rented stages and equipment from the larger companies such as Universal.

One stand-out performer during this era was the brunette Jacqueline Logan. Having gained acclaim through a Broadway revival titled *Floradora*, Jacqueline then began a successful tour as a Ziegfeld Follies girl. Hollywood beckoned and Jacqueline headed West to become a star in silent pictures. Unfortunately, the advent of sound would be Jacqueline's downfall, and she was finally forced into retirement in 1932.

Jacqueline is perhaps best remembered for her role in the first sound serial, Mascot Pictures' *King of the Kongo* (1929). Jacqueline's character is a lady who is seeking her lost father. With only a trinket left by him to guide her, she teams up with a secret service agent, who has found an identical trinket. Together, they travel to a temple where they encounter a gang of ivory thieves, a dangerous gorilla and a wide variety of nasty and unpleasant surprises. Undoubtedly it was classic B material!

In 1930, a strange jungle movie called *Ingagi* hit a barrage of censorship barricades due to faked gorilla footage and female nudity. *Ingagi*'s premise surrounded an expedition into Africa to investigate rumors of a gorilla-worshipping tribe of natives. As the result of being banned from theaters and other censorship problems, *Ingagi* got scads of free press because of the hype surrounding a scene with a topless native woman purportedly facing a virgin sacrifice. The filmmakers fought long and hard for distribution, and when *Ingagi* hit the theaters it pulled in bundles of money from curious audiences.

The African gorilla theme is a favorite of genre filmmakers. In 1932, *Savage Girl* hit the theaters. Starring lovely Rochelle Hudson, a classic beauty who would take on hard-hitting lead roles in the later 1930s and 1940s, the movie followed an expedition into Africa to find a white woman living with a gorilla. Adorned in a sexy leopard-skin outfit, Rochelle gave theatergoers lots of bang for their buck.

Speaking of big apes, in 1933 the film-going public would be introduced to the queen genre films goddess, Fay Wray, who would appear in both *King Kong* and *The Vampire Bat* that year. Fay Wray rocketed to stardom in 1928 with the tragic lead role in *The Wedding March*. Her first horror picture was *Doctor X* (1932) followed by *The Most Dangerous Game* (1932). One year later, Fay Wray would land the role that would not only typecast her but would ultimately result in a lifetime of fame and glory.

In *King Kong,* Fay Wray played Ann Darrow, an actress who traveled to Skull Island with a film crew for the filming of a movie. The natives cast their eyes on the blonde beauty and kidnap her for their sacrifice to the mysterious king of the island. Fay, her dress torn to shreds, is bound in chains outside the giant gate as natives beat their drums and the incessant chants of "Kong!" ring through the air. The tension builds as Ann sees the trees sway and part and the gigantic Kong comes into view. At which point Faye Wray releases the most blood-curdling scream, a scream that still reverberates to this very day. *King Kong* is a masterful blend of sexuality and horror—beauty and the beast. The terrified female, her slip peeking through the torn dress, is placed in a submissive state and surrounded by pulsating drums, as the audience is hypnotically lured into the erotic, primal jungle, while at the same time forced to the edge of their theater seats as the foreboding Kong approaches his gasping victim. *King Kong* may be the best example in which sex and horror become not two separate elements, but a united entity that draws upon the audience's hidden fantasies.

Fay Wray is terrorized once again in *The Vampire Bat*.

Fay Wray would again face grotesque perils in *The Vampire Bat*. In a small village in Central Europe villagers are being found dead—mysteriously drained of all their blood. As the suspense grows, and the paranoia of vampire bats builds, it is discovered that a mad doctor is using his assistant to kill the townsfolk in the name of science. Fay Wray plays Ruth, the doctor's second assistant, who becomes the inevitable damsel in distress.

George E. Turner and Michael H. Price cover Poverty Row films extensively in their excellent series *Forgotten Horrors: The Definitive Edition* (Midnight Marquee, 1999), *Forgotten Horrors 2* (Midnight Marquee, 2001) and *Forgotten Horrors 3* (Luminary Press, 2003). Turner and Price say of *The Vampire Bat*:

Fay Wray and Joel McCrea in *The Most Dangerous Game*

Producers were quick to discover that red-blooded males in the audience would have given their eye-teeth to be the lucky guy who protects Miss Wray...More than a real beauty, Miss Wray projects in films a quality of innocence that contrasts powerfully with madmen and monsters.

Fay Wray's career would span over 100 films. She married and retired in the early 1940s, then made a brief return to film in the 1950s. She also appeared in the 1980 TV movie *Gideon's Trumpet*. Fay Wray remains Hollywood and fantastic film royalty and has a devoted following of B film aficionados.

The 1930s Golden Age of Horror Films would shine the spotlight on a host of other great actresses. In 1932 silent screen actress Madge Bellamy appeared in her most memorable role as Madeline in *White*

Madge Bellamy and Bela Lugosi in *White Zombie*

Zombie. Traveling to Haiti for her wedding, she is turned into a zombie by Murder Legendre (Bela Lugosi) at the request of the smitten Mr. Beaumont (Robert Frazer). Though her character is extremely one-dimensional and her performance left much to be desired, her appearance as the beautiful zombie still haunts audiences.

Irish beauty Valerie Hobson was extremely busy in 1934-1936, appearing in films such as *The Man Who Reclaimed His Head* (1934), *Werewolf of London* (1935), *Chinatown Squad* (1935) and her most memorable role, Elizabeth Frankenstein in *The Bride of Frankenstein* (1935). In *The Bride of Frankenstein*, Hobson is taken hostage by Dr.

Valerie Hobson and Boris Karloff in *Bride of Frankenstein*

Pretorius (Ernest Thesiger), who uses her as leverage to force Henry Frankenstein (Colin Clive) to create a female companion for the Monster in this horrific science fiction sequel to *Frankenstein*. Universal had introduced *Frankenstein* to the world in 1931 and officially began the Golden Age of Horror. Mae Clarke was the token female and portrayed the frightened Elizabeth, fiancée of Henry Frankenstein (Colin Clive). *Frankenstein's* raw emotion, stunning performances and electrifying special effects left shrieking audiences wanting more.

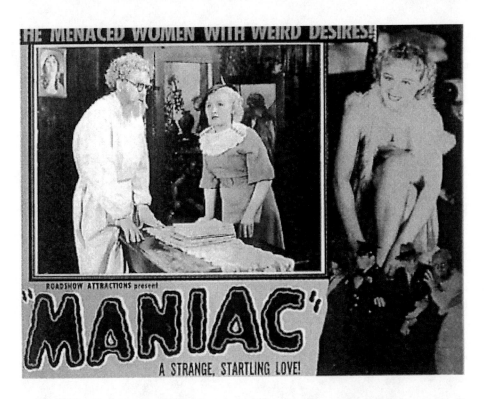

In 1934 the granddaddy of exploitation films would debut to shocked and appalled audiences. Director and producer Dwain Esper introduced the world to the outrageous *Maniac*, which traversed the boundaries and limits of good taste and immersed audiences into the demented world of Dr. Meirshultz (Horace Carpenter), a scientist intent—or better yet driven—to reanimate the dead. Following a series of gruesome scenes, the doctor tries to convince his assistant Maxwell (Bill Woods) to commit suicide so the doctor can revive Maxwell's corpse. Instead, Maxwell turns the gun on Meirshultz and kills him. The film then proceeds to spiral through the recesses of Maxwell's mind as he slowly goes insane and carries on the doctor's grisly compulsion to kill and then revive the dead.

Maniac and Esper happily broke every rule of the Hays Code, but Dwain Esper did not despair. In the true B entrepreneurial spirit Esper took *Maniac* (and most of his other movies) on the road, hitting road-houses and specialty theaters. Even more popular today than during Esper's heyday, *Maniac* was chock full of violence and gratuitous nudity, provided courtesy of a female cast that included Phyllis Diller, Thea Ramsey and Jennie Dark.

Frank Shannon, Jean Rogers, Richard Alexander and Jack Lipson in *Flash Gordon*

Science fiction would continue to build inroads in the 1930s with serials such as *Flash Gordon* starring Buster Crabbe. Burton Holmes in his article "Erotic Sci-Fi" notes:

> Scantily-clad damsels in distress were one of the ways Hollywood got boys and men into the theaters, and sci-fi serials were a medium that could make full use of them, as opposed to Western serials where the women were dressed from neck to ankle.

Jean Rogers as Dale Arden in this exciting serial had the annoying habit of fainting at the most inopportune moments, but ultimately she was a strong female character. *Flash Gordon* provided actresses with more heroic roles and helped Hollywood realize the appeal of stalwart female characters.

Helen Chandler and Bela Lugosi in *Dracula*

But it was those blood-sucking vampires that gave women a chance to sink their teeth into some juicy roles in the 1930s. Although the female vampires were controlled by the male vampire in the case of *Dracula*'s brides and the evil Sandor (Irving Pinchel) in *Dracula's Daughter*, the seductive women lent an air of forbidden eroticism to the horror film. Male audience members could happily ogle the vampire vixens and women could appreciate the film fantasy of controlling docile men with a mere vampire's kiss.

In 1931 director Tod Browning chose lovely Helen Chandler for the role of Dracula's female victim. While Chandler's heroine was the innocent, whose repressed sexuality was brought to the surface by the suave Count Dracula (Bela Lugosi), it would be Dracula's brides (Jeraldine Dvorak, Cornelia Thaw and Dorothy Tree), who represented unbridled lust.

Carroll Borland in *Mark of the Vampire*

Carroll Borland would portray the very intriguing vampire woman Luna in *Mark of the Vampire* (1935). Returning to familiar ground, Tod Browning had Bela Lugosi don the vampire mantle once more, this time as Count Mora, while Carroll Borland played his daughter. A friend of Lugosi's and a student at Berkeley College, Borland's appearance in *Mark of the Vampire* is one of the most visually memorable vampire sirens, her face still readily associated with horror films of the 1930s. While her

Gloria Holden and Irving Pinchel in *Dracula's Daughter*

performance is limited to slinking about the fog-shrouded set and glow-ering erotically, Carroll Borland almost succeeded in stealing the movie from Lugosi. Unfortunately, even Lugosi couldn't save the stodgy mystery and fake vampire story of *Mark of the Vampire* and Borland's acting career basically began and ended with Luna.

In 1936 Gloria Holden would star as *Dracula's Daughter*, which, although advertised as a sequel to *Dracula*, only allowed audiences to catch a glimpse of the supposed corpse of the famed Count. Holden plays Countess Zaleska, Dracula's daughter, who has come to London to claim her father's body. The dark-eyed Holden was able to give a poignant performance as Zaleska, alternating between a desire to free herself from Dracula's curse, while succumbing to the bloodlust of her vampirism. Unlike Carroll Borland, Gloria Holden continued with a successful acting career through 1958.

Bela Lugosi and Jacqueline Wells in *The Black Cat*

Other memorable female leads of the 1930s include Jacqueline Wells as the intended sacrificial victim in *The Black Cat* (1934), Marian Marsh in the dark fairy tale *The Black Room* (1935), and Frances Drake as the actress with a murderous admirer in *Mad Love* (1935) followed by her performance as Diane Rukh in the horror/sci-fi classic *The Invisible Ray* (1936). Fans of Scream Queens should not miss Midnight Marquee's *Hollywood's Classic Scream Queens: 1930s*, which is chock full of rare photos and portraits of 1930s genre beauties.

With World War II underway in Europe and the Pacific, the 1940s audiences sought escapist entertainment. Universal cashed in with Monster Rallies but new horror mavericks would arise at RKO—producer Val Lewton and his team of intelligent and talented directors. Two of the more famous films from the Lewton unit were *Cat People* (1942) and *I Walked with a Zombie* (1943).

In *Cat People*, the lovely Simone Simon would intrigue audiences with the question "was she or wasn't she one of the Cat People?" Simone's exotic beauty and cat-like features held audiences enthralled. She would return in 1944 for a follow-up in *The Curse of the Cat People*, which was directed by Robert Wise. Simone, with her wild social life, caused the Hollywood gossips to work overtime before she ultimately returned to her home in France after World War II.

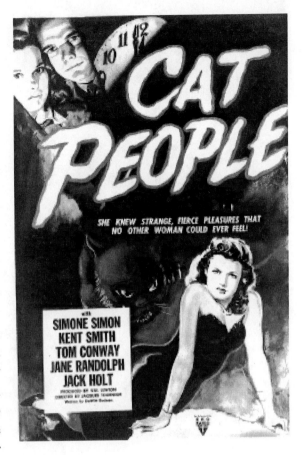

Frances Dee in *I Walked with a Zombie* was a young nurse who traveled to the West Indies to care for a woman stricken by a strange illness. As the title clued, the woman had in fact been turned into a zombie, and Dee—a veteran lead who would continue appearing in films through the 1950s—made the terrifying Lewton walk through the eerie swamp.

Although a large percentage of 1940s cinema featured patriotic films, which were meant to keep the up spirits of a despondent country, low-budget movies continued to do their part by providing a share of escapist entertainment. The horror circuit was filled with a variety of movies that included *The Monster and the Girl* (1941), in which Ellen Drew is the helpless heroine who is drawn into the dark evils of the big city. Her brother sets out to save her but winds up executed for murder, only to have his brain implanted into a gorilla. The gorilla eventually has its

Evelyn Ankers in *Captive Wild Woman*

revenge on the villains in this bizarre horror entry, which featured George Zucco as the experimenting scientist. In *Captive Wild Woman* (1943) with Evelyn Ankers and the exotic Acquanetta, a native woman is turned into a gorilla, which eventually reverts back to a violent, primal nature. *Weird Woman* (1944) offered Fritz Leiber's haunting tale of a college professor (Lon Chaney) and his island-born bride (Ann Gwynne), who are subjected to vicious attacks by the professor's spurned love (Evelyn Ankers). In *The Woman Who Came Back* (1945) Nancy Kelly portrays a New England woman who survives a bus crash only to face the terrors of a family curse based upon witchcraft. June Lockhart depicts another curse victim as the title character in the *She-Wolf of London* (1946). The talented and beautiful Gale Sondergaard, Sherlock Holmes' nemesis in *Spider Woman*, once again played with spiders in 1946's *Spider Woman Strikes Back*. She is an evil scientist using the blood of innocent girls in her experiments.

Evelyn Ankers and Elizabeth Russell in *Weird Woman*

Weird Woman, one of Universal's *Inner Sanctum* series, could be called a "Scream Queen Rally," which featured three of the brightest lights of 1940s horror.

Evelyn Ankers, born August 17, 1918 in Valparaiso, Chile, made her film debut with a bit part in *Rembrandt* (1936), which enabled her to work with legends Charles Laughton, Gertrude Lawrence and Elsa Lanchester. After appearing in a series of small roles, Ankers found eternal fame in the horror films of the 1940s. She was heroine Gwen Conliffe in Universal's *The Wolf Man* (1941), and according the film historian Gregory Mank, faced as many terrors actually filming the movie as her onscreen character faced in the film. Ankers' next horror outing was as Elsa in *Ghost of Frankenstein* (1942), followed by *The Mad Ghoul* (1943) with George Zucco, and once again she faced terrors both on- and off-

Anne Gwynne in *House of Frankenstein*

screen with Lon Chaney, Jr. in *Son of Dracula* (1943) and *The Frozen Ghost* (1945). Evelyn Ankers would appear in 38 films during the 1940s—mostly horror and B films—for which she was dubbed "The Screamer" or less politely by Hollywood insiders as "the poor man's Fay Wray."

Anne Gwynne also appeared in *Weird Woman* with her good friend Ankers. Gwynne would first appear in *The Unexpected Father* (1939) before becoming a staple in B Westerns and 1940s horror films. Originally from Texas, Gwynne signed with Universal at the age of 20. During the course of this decade she would appear in such fright fare as *Black Friday* (1940) with both Bela and Boris; *The Black Cat* (1941) with Bela and Basil Rathbone; *Weird Woman* (1944); monster rally *House of Frankenstein* (1944) with Boris, Lon Chaney, Jr., John Carradine, Lionel Atwill and George Zucco; and *The Ghost Goes Wild* (1947). Gwynne would eventually star in television's first filmed dramatic series, *Public Prosecutor* (1947/48).

Weird Woman's third fem was the always brilliant Elizabeth Russell. Born in 1916, Russell made her horror film debut in 1942's *The Corpse Vanishes*. She soon became part of the Lewton company, appearing in *The Cat People* (1942), *The Seventh Victim* (1943), *The Curse of the Cat People* (1944) and *Bedlam* (1946). Russell also appeared in the classic ghost film *The Uninvited* (1944), *Weird Woman* (1944), *Hitler's Madman* (1943) and *Youth Runs Wild* (1944).

In the 1950s, the Golden Age Monsters of the 1930s and 1940s and the subtle terrors of Val Lewton were ignored, as Hollywood discovered teenagers and atomic bombs. Drive-in theaters multiplied faster than rabbits and teenagers flocked to this parent-free haven of sex and horror. Moviemakers cranked out quickie B movies to appeal to the previously overlooked teen audience.

1950s sci-fi films played upon American fears of nuclear war and Commie invasions. In *Danse Macabre*, Stephen King elaborates on this theme by declaring, with much humility, that *Earth Vs. The Flying Saucers* (1956) has become the epitome of cold war statements. Beneath its campy tale of invaders from space, the movie becomes a "preview of the ultimate war." King, along with many other notable film historians, equates these spacemen and their flying saucers with the Russians that every good American feared,

Margaret Sheridan was the token love interest of Kenneth Tobey in *The Thing*.

and the annihilation of historic monuments, symbols of American freedom, become a vision of "the destruction one would logically expect when the A-bombs finally fly."

Two undisputed 1950s classics were *The Thing... From Another World* (1951) and *The Day the Earth Stood Still* (1951). In *The Thing*, a team of Air Force personnel and scientists discover a frozen alien, which quickly goes on a murderous rampage once it thaws out. Although the cast is primarily male, the token female Margaret Sheridan graced nearly every movie poster in one screaming state or another. In *The Day the Earth Stood Still*, a spaceman arrives on earth with a strong message that if the world doesn't change its war-mongering ways, total annihilation is eminent. Among the cast was Patricia Neal, who plays a young widow who must seek out the spaceman's robot with the instructions necessary to prevent it from destroying the world. Patricia Neal would later receive an Academy Award for her role in *Hud*.

1950s Hollywood would give birth to many fondly remembered aliens and sci-fi flicks including *Invaders from Mars* (1953), *Creature from the Black Lagoon* (1954), *The Quatermass Experiment* (1955/56), *This Island Earth* (1955) and *Forbidden Planet* (1956).

Forbidden Planet may have provided the first of the modern scream queens in the shapely form of Anne Francis as the nubile Altaira. A space ship lands on a planet where a group of space colonists are believed to have disappeared some 20 years previously. The crew discovers Robby the Robot, Dr. Morbius and his stunning daughter Altaira, who manages to turn the male crewmembers into lust-filled imbeciles—not to mention young male audience members mesmerized by Francis' subtle "nude" swimming scene and her seductive costumes.

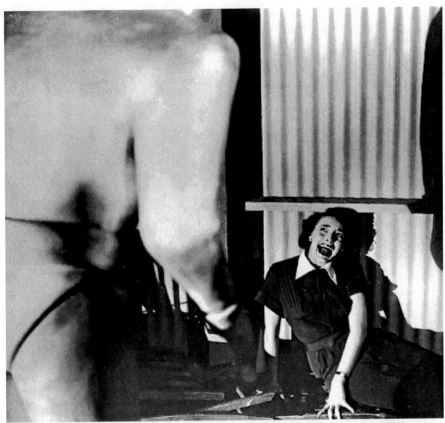

Patricia Neal as the heroine of *The Day the Earth Stood Still*

Often 1950s sci-fi films featured a slew of buxom alien beauties sprawling about in tight outfits on drapery covered boudoir-like sets. 1953's *Abbott and Costello Go to Mars* is the perfect example as A&C encounter Mari Blanchard as the Queen of Venus and ruler of many lovely ladies—including eight Miss Universe contestants. Also in 1953 *Cat-Women of the Moon* crept into theaters. The Cat-Women, including Carol Brewster, Susanne Alexander and Susan Morrow, wore form-fitting bodysuits, and used their hypnotic powers to control the male crew, but heroine Marie Windsor helps save them from the hell-cat women.

Devil Girl from Mars (1954) featured dominatrix alien Patricia Laffan menacing Hazel Court. Another cat-suited alien babe, Shirley Kilpatrick used her radiation touch to kill most of the cast in *The Astounding She-Monster* (1958). Meanwhile, Richard Cunha made the ultra-low budget *Missile to the Moon* in 1959, which was essentially a remake of *Cat-Women*. *Missile to the Moon* turned up the heat with a cast that included

...A GIANT FIENDISH CREATURE

MISSILE to the MOON

starring
RICHARD TRAVIS · CATHY DOWNS · K.T. STEVENS
TOMMY COOK co-starring NINA BARA · GARY CLARKE
MICHAEL WHALEN with Laurie Mitchell · Marjorie Hellen
Henry Hunter · Lee Roberts and featuring
The INTERNATIONAL BEAUTY CONTEST WINNERS

Cathy Downs, Nina Bara, *Playboy's* Marianne Gaba and seven other "International Beauty Contest Winners." These films would ultimately influence 1969's *Zeta One*, a soft-core sci-fi film, which showcased beauties Dawn Addams, Valerie Leon, Kirsten Betts and Yutte Stensgaard, who ultimately played strip-poker with the hero.

These 1950s films sought to target teenagers with tales of teen angst, juvenile delinquency and sci-fi. Mamie Van Doren, dubbed "the poor man's Marilyn Monroe," exploded onto the B film scene. With dyed, platinum blonde hair and a curvaceous body, Mamie made her way from bit parts at RKO to Universal where she was cast in a series of low-budget, drive-in films including *Running Wild* in 1955 and *Untamed Youth* in 1957. In *Untamed Youth*, Mamie and her sister wind up in jail but find time for four musical numbers that drove teenage audiences wild and had the censors reeling. Mamie then slithered into *High School Confidential!* (1958) starring Russ Tamblyn, who is seduced by Van Doren, who appears as his nymphomaniac aunt. Her next film was *The Beat Generation* (1959), a slapdash crime film featuring a rather esoteric cast including Jackie Coogan, Louis Armstrong, Irish McCalla, Vampira and Maxie Rosenbloom!

Attack of the B Queens

Other B film divas of the 1950s include Leigh Snowden in the otherwise forgettable *Hot Rod Rumble* (1957), Sandra Harrison as a troubled girl in *Blood of Dracula* (1957), and Gloria Castillo, Yvette Vickers and Luana Anders in *Reform School Girl* (1957). Mary Murphy received the admiration of biker stud Marlon Brando in the classic *The Wild One* (1954)

Lest we forget, we'll give a nod to savvy promoters who included teenager in their film titles. The list is extensive but notables include *I Was a Teenage Werewolf* (1957) with Yvonne Lime as the innocent girlfriend of Michael Landon, *I Was a Teenage Frankenstein* (1957) where Phyllis Coates became crocodile food, *Teenage Zombies* (1958) where Katherine Victor menaces a group of teens, and possibly the worst of all—*Teenagers from Outer Space* (1959), where Dawn Anderson became the love-interest of an invading alien.

Other actresses making their presence felt in B movies of the 1950s included Marilyn Nash as a strong-willed scientist in *Unknown World* (1951); Faith Domergue in *This Island Earth* (1955) and *It Came from Beneath the Sea* (1955); Barbara Lawrence in *Kronos* (1957), Mari Blanchard as a dying woman given a serum that makes her indestructible in *She Devil* (1957) and Mara Corday in *The Giant Claw* (1957) and *The Black Scorpion* (1957). Mara Corday also appeared in *Tarantula* (1955) with John Agar, which was a huge hit for Universal. She eventually was *Playboy*'s Miss October 1958, which used photos taken years before.

The innocent 1950s were coming to an end and film studios began to test the strict censor-imposed bonds of Hollywood with increased sex and violence—ultimately becoming the main ingredient of B cinema of the 1980s and 1990s. The beginning of the end was helped along by Russ Meyer, who would mastermind an array of archetypal B films. Having spent time photographing pin-up models for *Playboy*, he shot a nudie film at the request of several friends. Russ took a new approach, seeking to surround the sexual elements with a story he believed audiences would enjoy. In 1959 he premiered his first film, *The Immoral Mr. Teas*, which included a bare-chested June Wilkinson. He followed this with *Eve and the Handyman* (1960) featuring his future wife Eve Turner, and then cranked out a number of films including *Erotica* (1961), *Wild Gals of the Naked West* (1962), *Europe in the Raw* (1963) and his cult masterpiece, starring the voluptuous Tura Satana, *Faster, Pussycat! Kill! Kill!* Russ Meyer's success would inspire future B filmmakers to new heights of depravity.

On the more mainstream level, Roger Corman and Sam Arkoff would begin featuring cleavage-baring beauties in a series of horror and beach party movies, while Hammer Films would blaze the sexual film trail using models-turned-actresses in a series of horror films in the 1960s and 1970s. The die had been cast—and the clothes cast aside—and the scream queen entered the age of anything goes: it did, it does and it will continue.

THE CORMAN HEROINES
by Justine Elias

Making a film with Roger Corman has served as a boot camp for some of Hollywood's most prominent directors (Francis Ford Coppola, Jonathan Demme, James Cameron, Martin Scorsese and Ron Howard, to name a few), screenwriters (Robert Townsend), and producers (Gale Anne Hurd, Polly Platt). For actors like Jack Nicholson, Bruce Dern, Peter Fonda, Dennis Hopper, Oscar nominees all, early films for Corman's American International Pictures served as stepping stones to long careers. For women in front of the camera, though, the Corman credits on their resume didn't often bode so well; their early movies tend to be more memorable to fans.

A B movie heroine, even if the actress playing her had only a short career, is notable for what she did in those movies: she avenged, she escaped, she committed more than her share of crimes, she fought (or fought back) and she died screaming and yelling and cursing. Frequently she did so while wearing very little clothing, as though she'd forgotten, unlike the men in the movie, just how chilly the weather was that day, and she boldly preferred to go out of doors wearing nothing but her undergarments.

Right there in the costume department, any at-

Until now no one has dared to film this...the most diabolical classic of all time!

AMERICAN INTERNATIONAL PICTURES present

Edgar Allan Poe's

THE **PIT**

AND THE

PENDULUM

FILMED IN PANAVISION AND COLOR

"Down and still down it came — to cross the region of the heart!..." POE

VINCENT PRICE · JOHN KERR · BARBARA STEELE · LUANA ANDERS · SCREENPLAY BY RICHARD MATHESON · PRODUCED AND DIRECTED BY ROGER CORMAN · MUSIC BY LES BAXTER

tempt at a real feminist argument for these movies gets pretty much shot to hell.

But no matter how absurd the stories, no matter how flimsy (or nonexistent) the costumes, there was generally something cool as well as beautiful about the best of the Corman movie heroines. Cool—meaning she did stuff, she caused trouble and then worked her way out of it. Maybe that doesn't sound like much, but it's more remarkable than standing on the sidelines and weeping or applauding as the men do whatever they've got to do.

Even for a seemingly standard exploitation title like *The Student Nurses* (1970), Corman's first movie for New World Pictures, the producer himself insisted that the four hot-and-horny TLC-administering health care professionals "each had to work out her problems without relying on a boyfriend." Not a radical idea, filmmakers rarely acknowledge that even promiscuous eye candy can be more interestingly portrayed on film if they are shown to be, in the end, somewhat in charge of their lives, or at least able to question the status quo.

If you haven't met the best of these B movie heroines, it's time to get acquainted.

Dudley Dickerson and Beverly Garland in *The Alligator People*

BEVERLY GARLAND

Look closely at those deep brown eyes. You've seen them before, and often. The actress who stars as kind, sensible silver-blonde ladies on the WB's family drama *Seventh Heaven* and the daytime soap *Port Charles* and does guest spots on countless other TV series, is the same one who played loving stepmom to Fred MacMurray's boys on *My Three Sons*. There's something steady and comforting about Garland, and perhaps that's why producers and casting directors have been relying on her for more than 50 years. The native Californian also happens to be a successful hotel owner, running the Beverly Garland Holiday Inn in North Hollywood. Check out her website, www.beverlygarland.com. But early in her career, Hollywood saw something else in Garland: an outlaw. She joked to the *Toronto Star* that in her 20s and 30s, she was known for playing "whores, alcoholics and gunslingers." And sometimes all three at once.

In 1955's *Swamp Diamonds* (also known as *Swamp Women*), one of the four feature films in which she was directed by Corman, she plays

Vera, the leader of a band of tough female convicts. It's hardly a glamorous role, but then Women in Prison movies aren't about glamour...or serious exploration of the criminal code or conditions behind bars; they're about women getting in catfights as quickly and nakedly as possible. Why else would anyone see or make these films?

Give Corman some credit for innovation: he doesn't keep his jailbirds behind prison walls for long. The cons, plus an undercover policewoman in search of a hidden cache of jewels, escape into the bayou, where the humidity drives them to tie their shirts over their midriffs, roll up their tight jeans, and occasionally seize one another by the hair during the inevitable (in movies, anyway) girl on girl arguments. The bayou heat, it's just plain *sultry*. The unexpected appearance of a pre-*Mannix* Mike "Touch" Connors and his girlfriend only raises the tension further. Though the convicts attempt to seduce their male hostage at gunpoint, he manfully resists. Because these are vicious, hard-bitten criminals, they are torn apart by greed and lust (the movie's ad copy claims they are "Man Crazed" but please—in a women's prison movie? Doubtful.) One escapee gets eaten by an alligator, and the remaining two, Garland and Marie Windsor, fight it out as a poisonous snake threatens to bite Connors. When Garland goes to shoot the attacking snake, Windsor seizes her chance and kills Garland with a thrown spear.

I suppose you could say justice prevails: the policewoman reveals her true identity, and Connors falls madly in love with her. The symbolism with the snake and the spear, I'm not even going to touch that, okay?

Garland was similarly no-nonsense in *It Conquered the World* (1956). Though the poster promises lurid thrills ("Every Man Its Prisoner! Every Woman Its Slave!"), the movie's "It" turns out to be a big rubbery creature that looks like an overripe cucumber. We learn that It is from Venus and bent on global domination. Oddly, scientist Lee Van Cleef agrees to help. His friend Peter Graves tries to convince him that the

Beverly Garland and John Bromfield in Universal's *Curucu, Beast of the Amazon*

cucumber is rotten, but it's Garland, as the scientist's wife, who gets the best onscreen moment. Brandishing a rifle, she takes aim and yells, "You think you're going to make a slave of the world? I'll see you in hell first!"

It conquered a new generation of fans when *Mystery Science Theater 3000* heckled the movie during the show's third season with Comedy Central (1991-1992). Though the movie itself came in for some ruthless remarks, Garland became one of the show's favorite actresses. *MST3K*'s Paul Chaplin, in *The Mystery Science Theater Amazing Colossal Episode Guide*, notes that her character alone took a stand that the audience could relate to: "Married to an idiot, she...takes matters into her own hands. She finds the Venusian pickle and delivers a dressing down that had to leave the poor creature more than a little abashed. Unfortunately she's then eaten, but she goes down fighting and probably praying that she'll get stuck in the bastard's throat and choke him. In certain respects, it's a ridiculous scene. Yet she delivers her lecture with the

Beverly Garland and Ray Milland in *Not of This Earth*

strongest commitment you could ever hope for. In that moment, she *is* a woman enraged at a pickle. I mean this. It shows such pride to perform like that, and to make sure your characters all have pride."

Today, it is easy to laugh at 50-year-old science fiction movies, especially ones that were filmed, however ingeniously, on a shoestring budget. The dialogue between the scientist and his friend couldn't be more ponderous, and neither of the male stars seem quite human in their reactions to the situation.

That's a drawback of a lot of early science fiction, though. The focus is on the debates between scientists and military types, and the audience can never be convinced by reasons and remedies when people just like them (the teenagers, the women) are coming face to face with lethal, disgusting alien creatures. Cinema is rife with such dramatic conflicts, which tend to result in a great deal of shrieking and fleeing and falling and spraining of ankles. But not when Garland is onscreen. Where others would shrink away in terror, her character assesses the situation, forms a plan and acts on it. There's a freakishly large insect (or plant...or *something*) in the house, and her spouse refuses to remove it. She must act aggressively and decisively since no one else will. Once Garland's gone, *It Conquered the World* lurches to a dull conclusion, with Van Cleef torching the creature and Graves giving a dreary, moralizing speech about the folly of the cucumber's plan—as if we didn't know before we'd seen the movie that space monsters haven't got our best interests at heart.

While the women Garland portrays have a sense of humor, the actress herself never appears to winking at the audience or to be laughing at the movie she is in. As *MST3K*'s Chaplin notes, Garland's "women always have spine and zing, and obvious integrity to go with the undeniable beauty." Nowhere are those qualities more on display than in *The Gunslinger*, written and directed by Corman in 1956. A meandering tale of Old West vengeance and upended gender roles, *Gunslinger* opens with the assassination of a frontier marshal. Without batting an eye, his devoted wife, Rose (Garland, of course) seizes a rifle and shoots back. (Are you detecting a pattern here?) At her husband's graveside, Rose demands justice, asking "Is there a man here who can handle the job?" Dead silence. Crickets chirp. Nervous glances all around. Really, it's quite an embarrassing moment.

So Rose nominates herself as her husband's replacement/avenger, trades in her frock for cowboy clothes, and goes in search of the assassins. Along the way, she teams up with a sinister but adequately attractive outlaw played by John Ireland. "Let's make a deal," leers Ireland. "I'll won't try to make you a bad woman if you stop trying to make me into a good man." By this time, Rose is willing to sleep with the guy (offscreen—it was the '50s after all) but not to trust him, she replies, "You're not bad. You're just no good." The expression on Rose's face just then, a look of sadness and resignation, tells you that she knows her new boyfriend is somehow going to fail her. When he turns out to be in the pay of the assassins ("Hired to kill the woman he loves," according to the movie's advertisements), Rose has to gun him down and ride off into the sunset. Because *Gunslinger* was made on the cheap, with a total of perhaps five horses and zero people who felt comfortable riding them, Rose's triumphant gallop into the sunset is instead a timid trot down a muddy path...a path that is marked by modern automobile tire tracks, if I'm not mistaken. Despite the poster's tagline, it's Garland, not Ireland, who turns out to be the title character.

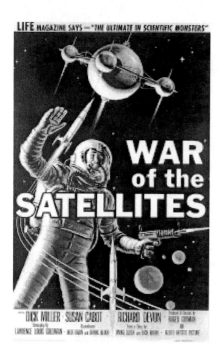

LIFE MAGAZINE SAYS – "THE ULTIMATE IN SCIENTIFIC MONSTERS"

WAR of the SATELLITES

DICK MILLER · SUSAN CABOT · RICHARD DEVON

SUSAN CABOT

Corman's subsequent heroines were rarely as admirably tough as Garland. In 1959's *The Wasp Woman*, Susan Cabot played an unusually powerful character for that time: the boss and spokeswoman of her own cosmetics company. Unfortunately, she's a parody of the manipulative, ball-busting female executive. Obsessed with youth and beauty, she's willing to dose herself with insect-derived elixir that makes her a murderous fiend. Cabot's screen machinations were not limited to the boardroom, either. In *Machine Gun Kelly* (1958), she was a slinky gangster's moll who effortlessly dominated the neurotic gangster-hero (a young Charles Bronson). In *Sorority Girl* (1957) Cabot was not a collegiate sister but the conniving rich girl who ruins the lives of all the other pledges.

Ray Milland and Hazel Court star in *Premature Burial*

HAZEL COURT

Britain's Hazel Court, who has the distinction of being a star for both Hammer and American International, brought a patrician beauty to her performances in Corman's Edgar Allan Poe films. In these, the most artistically ambitious of Corman's long list of movies, she embodied murderous greed (1964's *The Premature Burial*, opposite Ray Milland) and aristocratic cravenness (1964's *The*

Attack of the B Queens

Yvette Vickers sees the wrath of the *Attack of the 50 Ft. Woman*.

Masque of the Red Death). With Court on the guest list in *Masque*, being locked in a castle with decadent aristocrats seemed creepily alluring, but there's no excuse for what her character did to scaredy-cat Ray Milland in *Burial*.

YVETTE VICKERS

Attack of the Giant Leeches (1959) is a movie that terrified and confused me when I first saw it at the age of six. The giant leeches part, I got that. But I didn't get why the slovenly swamp-dwelling old man was being so mean to his adolescent granddaughter and her boyfriend. He always seemed to be yelling at her, and she was forever answering him back while writhing around in her underwear.

But then, a small child shouldn't comprehend what was actually going there. (A small child should not see this movie, either.) Even grownups can't quite believe what they're seeing in a horror movie that begins with the creepy May/late-December union between a jealous geezer (Bruno Ve Sota) and his trampish, sneaky teenage wife (Yvette Vickers).

When the giant leeches slither onscreen, it's almost a relief. Yet Vickers, a petite, blonde *Playboy* playmate of 1959, who would go on to play the sexy husband-stealer Honey Parker in *Attack of the 50 Ft. Woman*, was scarily on-target in her performance in this bayou-bound *Baby Doll*. Unfortunately, the actress didn't end up in better movies, or at least do more roles that showcased the sort of perverted sensuality she demonstrated in *Leeches*. After a stint as a *Reform School Girl* (1957), Vickers ended up playing parts like "Blond Yoga Girl" in the Avalon-Funicello romp *Beach Party* (1963).

CLAUDIA JENNINGS

She made only a handful of films before her death in a car accident at the age of 29, but for a few years Claudia Jennings reigned as a drive-in goddess, as roguish and believably athletic as a young Burt Reynolds. Often cast as one of a pair (or trio) of sisters on cheerful crime spree, she was in the bank-robbery comedy *The Great Texas Dynamite Chase* (bank robbery), *Moonshine County Express* (moonshine), and *'Gator Bait* (poaching alligators). Her first job for Corman was *Unholy Rollers* (1972), playing a bored factory worker looking for glory in the roller derby. As in so many sports movies (or early Burt Reynolds movies, for that matter), the heroine refuses to listen to her coach or cooperate with her teammates, but the fans love her anyway. The experience must have prepared her well for the *Mad Max in Thunderdome*-precursor *Deathsport* (1978), in which she and Jan-Michael Vincent play futuristic gladiators. Sadly, the movie was released just a few months before she died.

PAM GRIER

There's not enough ink to give Pam Grier her due as a B movie icon, but it's important to note that before she was the leading woman in Blaxploitation cinema, she too started with Corman. Among her early credits: three stints behind bars in early '70s women's prison movies. She was the fiercest prisoner in *The Big Bird Cage* (1971), *Women in Cages* (aka *Women's Penitentiary II,* also *I* 1972) and *The Big Doll House* (1972). The Philippines-filmed *The Big Bird Cage* serves up the standard women in prison routine—the requisite tortures and shower scenes, nasty locals and short-shorts clad prison matrons as the women's worst oppressors. Roberta Collier, who appeared in *Women in Cages* and *Caged Heat,* is the sort-of innocent heroine, while Grier plays a hardened inmate named Grear. Though Grier's characters (here and *Big Doll House*) suffer a fate similar to that of Beverly Garland's character in *Swamp Diamonds,* she does show her mettle by brawling with another inmate and making a none-too-subtle pass at the new inmate. By the way, that's Grier singing the movie's title theme at the start of the film.

GLAM BABES
FROM OUTER SPACE
by James Singer

For the past three decades, alleged UFO abductees under hypnosis have described their hosts as pale, large-eyed beings that resemble taller, thinner versions of the Pillsbury Dough Boy, an image adapted by Spielberg for his *Close Encounters of the Third Kind.* Nothing could be further from the truth.

Hypnotize any one of several low-budget Hollywood producers of the 1950s or '60s and scrutinize their UFO encounters. From such minds, researchers have learned what extraterrestrials really look like: tall, brilliant and beautiful women adept at blasting mutants, managing nuclear fusion labs and piloting space ships, all the while performing these exacting duties dressed in body-hugging swimsuits, ultra miniskirts and high heels. In short, centerfolds for *Scientific American.*

Despite claims of the government and scientific communities with their billion-dollar, yet flawed, space probes, it's well known that our solar system is inhabited by various Amazonian

The stuff that (men's) dreams are made of—*The Cat Women of the Moon*

super civilizations. For the serious student of cinematic history, this should come as no surprise. In fact, these revelations were fully documented over 30 years ago by such movie studios as Astor and Universal.

The concept of a society inhabited by attractive and seemingly available women is itself a myth as old as mankind and the message within this myth is that the female of the species is more deadly than the male. In Greek and Roman mythology, the Sirens, actually part woman and part bird, lured sailors to a watery death by seducing them with ethereal singing. In Greek mythology, the Amazons were a race of tough female warriors who removed one breast to improve their archery skills. The Amazon river in South America was named by the Spaniards who believed that such women lived near its shores, the word Amazon derived from *a* (without) *mazos* (breast).

Whatever the myriad variations on men entering an isolated colony of females, it's basically the stuff of age-old male sexual fantasies (which skin mag publishers Hugh Hefner and Bob Guccione created and fulfilled in real life). It was only natural that these wet-dreams and essen-

The elegant sci-fi costumes for *World Without End* were designed by Alberto Vargas.

tially adolescent fantasies would transfer well from lost islands, hidden jungles, ancient cultures and uncharted lands to the planets and moons in our solar system as a subject for pulp fantasy publications, men's adventure mags, paperbacks (with their lushly drawn cover paintings) and motion pictures. Women don't make movies or write books about all-male societies discovered by female explorers and they probably never will.

Many of the "good-girl" pin-up artists of the 1940s and 1950s were heavily enamored of the otherworldly images of beautiful young girls from other planets or from the future and their work can be seen in scores of men's mags, particularly during the '50s and early '60s, the dawn of true space exploration. The renowned Alberto Vargas of *Esquire* and later *Playboy* fame drew the set sketches and designed the futuristic cocktail-style dresses worn by the women of a post-nuclear war colony for *World Without End* (Allied Artists, 1956), a handsomely produced sci-fi adventure written and directed by Edward Bernds.

During the late 1940s and early 1950s, the flying saucer craze erupted. Outside the boundaries of serious investigation were UFO devotees, who,

like 20th-century descendants of the Baron Munchausen, told of trips in saucers to other planets and encounters, some sexual, with erotically exotic female aliens. Several of these claimants, George Adamski for one, became "stars" on the UFO lecture circuit. A few even developed a cult corps of believers, several of which remain in existence today, especially in South America.

Of course, these "true adventures" sounded not unlike the storylines from scores of science fiction/weird fantasy magazines and comic books. Irritating to professional UFO researchers, but fascinating to enthusiasts of the fantastic, UFO and strange phenomena publications and books sold well.

Predictably, these interplanetary recounts fell into the capable, if trembling, hands of numerous movie producers, ever on the lookout for way-out, exploitable subject matter that fit into that crowd-pleasing "spicy" realm. Stories of beautiful, scantily clad women living on distant worlds were a natural to fulfill their own box office dreams. So where are the absent male inhabitants of these societies in some of these films? Who knows? Who cares? The audience put their money down to see sexy outer space gals running around in revealing outfits with lots of leg show-

MARTIAN SCIENTIST FALLS FOR EARTHMAN! in *Flight to Mars*

ing, and maybe a cat fight or two thrown into the plot. If they were lucky.

While earlier comic strips and movies about the adventures of Flash Gordon and Buck Rogers invariably featured space sirens, the most memorable being Ming's daughter Princess Aura (Priscilla Lawson) in the Gordon shows, it wasn't until the post-war years that the space babe concept really went into full swing.

In *Flight to Mars* (Monogram, 1951), filmed in the two-strip Cinecolor process, an American rocket crew that included Arthur Franz and Cameron Mitchell discovered an advanced race of Martians. While the men of Mars were boring corporate types concerned with the dwindling of their natural resource, Corium, Martian babe scientist Marguerite Chapman bothered not with protective work uniforms when aiding Franz in his rocket repairs. Instead she and the producers preferred the revealing micro-dress popular that year on the Red Planet. Far from being the imperious female alien who would surface shortly in upcoming films, Marguerite's a regular Martian girl-next-door who, of course, falls for Franz and helps him and his team return to Earth.

Abbott and Costello Go to Mars **and meet Venusian beauties.**

1953 was a big year for all-female space societies. Movie-goers saw *Abbott and Costello Go to Mars* (Universal-International), although Bud and Lou actually bypassed Mars for an encounter with actress Mari Blanchard, the stunning Queen Allura of Venus, and her society of decoratively garbed Venusians. Blanchard was perfectly cast; in her heyday she had the face, form and bearing of a goddess.

Bud takes an all-too-brief recess from slapping his partner around to explore some social possibilities with the many starlets cast, among them eight Miss Universe contestants including Miss USA, Jackie Loughery, and Miss Sweden, Anita Ekberg, who was seven years away from wading in a Roman fountain with Marcello. Allura takes a jealous shine to Lou, preferring his brand of chubby virility to Abbott's mustachioed sleaze. Costello naturally must botch things with his kid-in-a-candy-store roving eye, causing the hot-tempered Queen to throw the boys and their two moronic mobster companions out of Venus and back into space.

Though not one of the true classic A&C films, I feel that *Go to Mars*, directed by series regular Charles Lamont, remains the most entertaining entry of the comedy team's '50s movies. The Venus-world section itself has a wonderfully surrealistic pulp paperback look in set and costume design due to Universal's highly talented craftspeople. The handsomely shot silvery movie would have been truly cotton candy for the eyes had it been photographed in color. Blanchard's regal crown weighed a mighty 14 pounds and caused her no small discomfort. Shop carpenters rigged up a rope-operated traction board to alleviate Mari's neck and back distress between takes, the gizmo resembling a cross between something out of a miniature gallows and a punishment device drawn by bondage artist Eric Stanton.

That same year, the *Cat-Women of the Moon* (Astor) used their paranormal feline powers to make life difficult for somnolent Sonny Tufts and tough guy Victor Jory. Originally shot in 3D, and later retitled *Rocket to the Moon* for television, this entry has an affectionate following. Wearing black bodysuits and tight wigs, the Cat-Women Alpha (Carol Brewster), Zeta (Susanne Alexander), Lambda (Susan Morrow) and the

Hollywood Cover Girls hypnotically controlled the already tigerish Earthwoman Marie Windsor, who was usually made of tougher stuff in her trenchcoat and bullet movies.

Living beneath the lunar landscape with some badly overweight spiders, the Cat-Women use their abundance of gold deposits as bait to knife one dollar-minded crewman. This not being a Universal production, budgetary constraints necessitated the use of office desk chairs and other cheapo substitutes for the rocket's control room set. *Cat-Women*'s hard-boiled dia-

logue, deadpan sincerity of its melodramatics and overheated acting, especially by the always entertaining Jory, give the film a lively charm.

Long before the gagwriters at television's *Mystery Science Theater 3000* got their hands on movies like *Cat-Women*, the reviewers at *The Hollywood Reporter* and *Variety* gave it a straightforward thumbs-up. "...Imaginatively conceived and turned-out science fiction yarn should get a good play in the s-f and exploitation market," wrote Whit of *Daily Variety*.

It was at this time that English filmmakers also heeded the call of pseudo-science exotica. However, their space gal films lacked the bachelor pad, men's mag pin-up allure of their American cousins, and ultimately suffered from those interminable scenes of endless conversations in pubs and drawing rooms that were the trademark of dozens of British science fiction films.

Devil Girl from Mars (Spartan, 1954) featured the imperious Patricia Laffan and her refrigerator-shaped robot bodyguard menacing future Hammer/AIP heroine Hazel Court and co-stars amidst a placid Scottish countryside setting. In a fetishistic costume straight out of another Eric

The Fire Maidens of Outer Space **were more the English rose types.**

Stanton dominatrix illustration, *Devil Girl* flew in to capture males for breeding experiments, another sexual fantasy rife in alien abductee case histories of the past 30 years. One wonders how films like this may have influenced the people who seriously claim these bizarre experiences.

On the flip side of the platter, the *Fire Maidens of Outer Space* (Topaz, 1956) were demure, fragile English rose types. Descendants of Atlantis, they live on one of Jupiter's moons and are in need of manly protection from a lecherous monster roaming their lovely gardens. American actor Anthony Dexter (star of *Valentino*, 1951) and his flight crew provide this beefcake bodyguarding, saving heroine Susan Shaw and galpals by dumping the Jupiterian horndog into a flaming pit. Like *Devil Girl, Fire Maidens* was written and played dead-straight, without a stitch of humor.

During the heyday of British sexploitation film production, the Brits released the sci-fi comedy *Zeta One* (aka *The Love Factor* aka *Alien Women*, 1969) in which a Bondian secret agent battled a society of alien beauties invading Earth to get men. Based on an adult comic strip, the rowdy *Zeta One* starred a bevy of Hammer Film beauties: Dawn Addams, the well-endowed Valerie Leon, Kirsten Betts and Danish actress Yutte Stensgaard (Carmilla/Mircalla the vampire in *Lust for a Vampire*, 1970), who plays a round of strip poker with the spy-hero.

In charting the cinematic history of Amazonian alien cultures, one discovers that Bud and Lou's hijinks on planet Venus had apparently culminated in some type of political upheaval, for in *Queen of Outer Space* (Allied Artists, 1958) tough but fair Mari Blanchard is out as queen and superbad girl Laurie Mitchell is in, with scientist Zsa Zsa Gabor aiming to depose her. Shot in CinemaScope and luminous colors, *Queen* also has a stirring music score by Marlin Skiles that melds celestial sounds with military motifs and even some *avant garde* jazz. The best known and most entertaining of all the wild, wild astro-bachelor/space girl pictures, the genesis of *Queen* has been attributed to a party joke by journalist Ben Hecht.

In an interview with Tom Weaver, director Edward Bernds (of Stooges/Bowery Boys fame) said that Hecht had written a 10-page outline, *Queen of the Universe*, which was brought to Allied by producer Walter Wanger. Hecht's basic idea, a planet controlled by women (he probably saw *A&C Go to Mars*), was turned into a working screenplay by the talented Charles Beaumont, later a stalwart for Rod Serling's *Twilight Zone*. Bernds and a co-writer spoofed up Beaumont's script. Giving a nod to *Go to Mars*, beauty queen contestants, notably Tania Velia, Miss Belgium, along with gorgeous actresses Lisa Davis and Barbara Darrow were cast as Venusians

Queen Yllana's mini-skirted army confronts traitor Zsa Zsa Gabor in *Queen of Outer Space***.**

Badly burned by radiation caused by the wars of Venusian males (a key plot device), Queen Yllana hides her disfigurement, but not her vicious temper, behind a mask. With her lovely mini-skirted army—the plain-looking girls must be under house arrest or something—Yllana dreams of pulverizing Earth with the very shaky-looking Beta Disintegrator, but not before putting her four male visitors through their paces.

Space trailboss Eric Fleming, sedentary scientist Paul Birch, wisecracker Dave Willock, and wolfish Patrick Waltz crash land courtesy of *World Without End* stock shots, are mugged by that always irritable big spider and are generally pushed around by the "Wicked Queen and her posse" before they overthrow her with the help of Gabor and her rebels. Mitchell is radiated to a horrible crisp by her own machine—strong stuff for its time—and the boys decide to hang with the Venusian vixens until whenever. Something of a pain in the ass to Bernds during filming, the annoying Gabor apparently is the only space lady in motion picture history to learn English by monitoring Hungarian radio waves.

When the guards in *Queen* stick their ray guns in the Earthmen's faces, they repeatedly bark out the order "Bachino!," no doubt Venusian for "move it" or something like that. You would think. According to one dictionary of international "dirty" words, "bachino" is a regional Italian slang word for fellatio. Whatever the reason for using this particular word in the script, it does change the movie's perspective a bit.

A formidable figure in a glowing, skintight body suit, Shirley Kilpatrick as *The Astounding She-Monster* (AIP, 1958) killed off most of the cast and one fuzzy bear with her touch of radioactive death, an unusual approach for an alleged peace delegate from outer space. Wordy geologist Robert Clarke figures out how to terminate the shapely invader with the lightning bolt eyebrows in record time since this is a 59-minute ultra-low-budget picture. One of the most fantastic looking alien femmes in movie history regardless of budget, the astounding Miss Kilpatrick was photographed walking backwards in several scenes to mask a split up the back of her second-skin costume.

A striptease dancer and nude model, Kilpatrick herself was not the model for the film's neat poster, intriguingly illustrated by the great Albert Kallis. Contemporary artist and psychotronic movie historian Jimmy Zero says that Madeleine Castle, a *Playboy* centerfold, provided the ac-

tual inspiration of *The Astounding-She Monster*'s uniquely stylized poster pose.

Director of *She Demons*, one of the all-time favorite monster chiller horror programmers, Richard Cunha shot *Missile to the Moon* (Astor, 1959) in one week for $60,000. A remake of Astor's *Cat-Women* (with some alterations), made as a co-bill with Cunha's *Frankenstein's Daughter*, this quickie starred Cathy Downs, Nina Bara and eight—count 'em—"International Beauty Contest Winners," among them *Playboy*'s Marianne Gaba. It must have been like homecoming week for space bad girls Laurie Mitchell and Tania Velia, here billed as Miss Yugoslavia.

The crew now consists of two rocket scientists (no pun intended), one fiancée, and two juvenile delinquent stowaways. It wasn't the same prop as in *Cat-Women*, but that darn giant spider was still present, a performer who surely deserved his own SAG card after all those screen appearances. Gumby-like Rock Men now also roamed the Lunar surface, trolling for astronauts, although it's clear that a 95-year-old cat woman could easily outrun them. A clip of the rocking Rock Men going after those nice Earth people was edited into the compilation film *It Came from Hollywood* (Paramount, 1982).

Astor wanted a sexier look so the cat-women's fashion sense had changed, abandoning their slinky black leotards for the interplanetary diaphanous look popular on Venus. The slanted eyebrows and tight wigs remained. They and their queen, now called the Lido, plot to leave the Moon in the Earth spaceship. As nasty as her predecessors, cat-woman Alpha knifes the Lido in the back. "The Lido has met with... an accident," she intones, clearly a student of the Costa Nostra school of do-it-yourself job promotion.

The violence quotient is raised in this version. The ubiquitous spider pounces on a screaming moon maiden and eats her, Alpha gets a knife in

her chest by her own hand, and all the cat girls die in terror when the air is released from their underground headquarters by an explosion. The climactic scene in which an astronaut is fried to a skeletal crisp by the lunar sunlight was also fairly gruesome in its day and was later edited out of most television prints.

From Mexico came *La Nave De Los Monstruous/The Ship of the Monsters* (Prod. Sotomayor S.A., 1959), a wacky little oddity that made the rounds of those infamous kiddie matinees of the early 1960s in urban theaters that were flea pits long before they were converted to flea markets. Mexican movie sex symbols Ana Bertha Lepe and Lorena Velazquez blast off their all-female planet to rocket Earthward with a robot assistant in tow. Clad in the obligatory swim suits and high heels, the statuesque pair waylay a singing vacquero, played by Lalo "Piporro" Gonzalez.

Besides engaging in several musical numbers (excruciating even for a six-year-old, let alone an infantile adult) with Senor Piporro, the aliens also control a menagerie of Halloween-style creatures that display a pretty salacious interest in the two sexpots. Lorena becomes a vampire (!) and takes over the ship, but winds up with a traditional stake through the heart while Piporro and Ana find romance. Now here's a picture with

Only in Hollywood could super alien babes Gloria Victor and Delores Reed end up with Bob Ball and Frankie Ray in *Invasion of the Star Creatures*.

something for everyone. As in *Cat-Women* and *Missile*, the girls have Greek alphabet names (Gamma and Beta). Velazquez later went on to star in the knuckle sandwich series of Wrestling Women monster movies. *La Nave* is just as delirious as those gonzoid films and the Santo pictures she also appeared in. The surprisingly sleek, spacious design of the ship's bridge included an elevator tube, a spiral staircase and large, gyroscopic "generators," a more impressive set than in any of the American films in this chapter.

Invasion of the Star Creatures (AIP, 1962) was close to the end of the line for the glamour babes from space movies. Bruno VeSota, the family-sized character actor from a dozen Roger Corman features, directed *Star Creatures* with a mini-budget of $25,000. *Star Creatures'* original screenplay, written by Roger Corman regulars Dick Miller and Jonathan Haze (*Little Shop of Horrors*), had been initially rejected by Corman. The final screenplay credit went to Haze.

Definitely a guilty little pleasure but nothing to be ashamed over, *Star Creatures* was a static, extended burlesque skit, using the kind of

Greta Thyssen is driving John Agar crazy in *Journey to the Seventh Planet*.

comedy routines that exotic dancers and baggy-pants comics used to perform for groaning drunks in the strip joints. Blonde Gloria Victor and brunette Delores Reed, actresses of epic dimensions, played aliens-in-hotpants Dr. Puna and Prof. Tanga, a very unsubtle play on words. Their dubious plans for invasion included growing an army of plant creatures (Vega-men) in garden pots in a cave hideout near an army base.

As goldbricking soldiers, the leering, close to drooling comedy duo of Bob Ball and Frankie Ray trip up those plans between doing impressions of Lugosi and Cagney, and tossing smutty wisecracks at the superstacked Puna and Tanga. Barely tolerant of these little wiseguys, the film's end sees both formerly dominant alien scientists turn into trophy-babe girlfriends for the two idiots. Yes, in the movies, a scriptwriter's impossible dream can become a reality. Squeezed by the budget, VeSota's Vega-men costumes were made from tights and burlap sacks, and the make-do sets were totally threadbare. Yet Bruno was fortunate (extremely fortunate) in the casting of the physically impressive Victor and Reed.

Our silver screen friend John Agar and his cosmo-companions made a *Journey to the Seventh Planet* (AIP, 1962) and found a group of alluring fantasy women (Greta Thyssen, Ann Smyrner and friends) in settings reminding them of home; all were just mental illusions constructed by an enormous and pissed-off Uranian brain. The *Reptilicus* man, Sid Pink, shot this in Denmark, his then-base of operations. A picture that's been knocked around in print, some of *Journey*'s plot devices would turn up on such science fiction shows as *Lost in Space* and *Star Trek* years later.

In 1968, Corman combined elements of the 1962 Russian sci-fi movie *Planet of Storms* (aka *Planeta Burg*) with beachside footage of clam-shell-bikinied Mamie Van Doren and her all-female clan of psychic Venusians—directed by "Derek Thomas" (Peter Bogdanovich)—to form the cut 'n' paste *Voyage to the Planet of Prehistoric Women* for AIP's television arm.

One would think that, over the years, the porn film world would have latched on to the idea of an all-women planet or female alien visitors and would have screwed the theme into the ground. Such entries are actually difficult to find with the exception of *Star Virgins* (VCX, 1979) and *Ultraflesh* (Collectors, 1980), starring Seka and Serena. One reason is that the pulpishly imaginative space girl fantasies were meant to tease and titillate and that's not the objective of hardcore pornography.

Softcore exploitation producer David F. Friedman, however, did knock off a cheap little number called *Space Thing* (EVI, 1968), directed by Byron Mabe and starring the aptly named "Paula Pleasure" as a fiercesome rocketship mistress who dallies with her female crewmates and male visitors. All of it is the dream of a bored husband.

The Three Stooges featurette *Space Ship Sappy* (Columbia, 1957) brought the boys to a planet of alien jungle girls (with fangs yet), and Dolly Parton went off the wall in the *Saturday Night Live* TV skit, "Planet of the Gigantic Hooters." Spoofing up a genre that already contains a naturally inherent amount of tongue-in-cheek humor means going back to the source. *Amazon Women on the Moon* (Universal, 1987), a John Landis presentation, faithfully recreated the now superdated look, color scheme, style and corn of *Queen* in a brief, good-natured parody, with exotic action actresses Sybil Danning well-cast as Queen Lara and Lana Clarkson as her handmaiden Alpha Beta.

Edited among the various all-star vignettes and short films as a chopped-up, milkman's matinee TV movie, the *Amazon* segment had all the by now cliched elements: string-held rocket model; dead-on stock music; leggy, spear-carrying moon maids; a granite-jawed hero; the

Brooklynese joker *a la* Dave Willock; and location filming at good old Bronson Canyon. Directed by Robert K. Weiss, the *Amazon* movie clips are an affectionate tip of the hat to a departed fantasy genre that may have been chauvinistic in outlook regarding the role of the sexes, but was never mean-spirited or vulgar in execution. The same can't be said for the countless movies made over the last 20 years in which the female characters are either bikini bimbos, out to make money washing cars, screaming victims of male psycho-maniacs, or car-washing bikini-bimbos graphically murdered by psychomaniacs.

Lana Clarkson models a costume from *Amazon Women on the Moon.*

And it remains a type of film that has yet to ever completely run out of steam. Unlike the innuendo-loaded, conservative '50s, the sexual elements can be pumped up today for direct-to-cable and video sales. The lame teen comedy *Dr. Alien* (aka *I Was a Teenage Sex Mutant,* 1989) casts busty, baby-dollish Judy Landers as an extraterrestrial posing as a biology teacher and using one of her students for sex experiments. Objective? You guessed it: the old breeding game. In Ted Bohus' *Vampire Vixens from Venus* (Shanachie, 1995), centerfolds/actresses J.J. North, Leslie Glass and Therese Lynn play aliens who take shapely human shape to drain Earth boys of their sex energies. Bohus made the picture on a budget of only $200,000, which in these inflationary times is a brutally difficult feat to accomplish.

Personally, I look forward to the day when Kevin Costner will remake *Queen of Outer Space* with Sharon Stone for $200 million. Nothing is impossible in Hollywood, where they keep watching the skies for heavenly inspiration.

SCREAM QUEENS HAMMER STYLE:
The British Invasion
by Linnea Quigley

When Hammer Films began the journey that would give it the reputation as the foremost producer of Gothic-style horror films, the concept and image that today we associate with the term Scream Queen hadn't really been coined or conceived, along with the aspects that are part of the image.

In the 1950s the horror or sci-fi heroine (or female interest) or the supporting female character (or female interest) or, in some cases, the bad girl (or *female interest*!) was written for the following reasons:

a. To give the hero someone to save
b. Serve as a subordinate or ask the male lead what was going on
c. Be the romantic interest
d. Provide temptation (one of the best examples being Yvette Vicker's (Honey Wilder) in *Attack of the 50 Ft. Woman*, proving once more that a well-filled tight sweater beats a bed-sheet bikini almost every time!) or
e. Serve as Monster Fodder
f. Oh yes…SCREAM A LOT!

Every so often the female character was someone of equal or, once in a great while, greater accomplishments than the hero (a scientist or an expert in a particular field). Occasionally, the female character would be the one investigating mysterious goings on (such as Beverly Garland in *The Alligator People*). But on the whole, the main purpose of the female character was pretty much the same as it had been since the silents of the 1920s.

Hammer Films was no exception in its early productions. In *The Quatermass Experiment* [*The Creeping Unknown* in the U.S.] (1956), Margia Dean's anxious Judith Caroon was usable up to a point, then was sent into screaming mode. Of course, seeing your alien-possessed husband's right arm turned into a swollen, spine-covered amalgam of human limb and a cactus would be enough to put anyone over the edge. In *Quatermass II* [*Enemy From Space*] (1957), barmaid Vera Day

Hazel Court as the innocent Elizabeth in *The Curse of Frankenstein*

was decorative, saucy, sexy (for that time and as much as the censor would allow) and lasted for only 10-15 minutes (about two-thirds of the way into the film) before becoming a victim of invading alien organisms. Yet, she was featured in the ads and posters for the film. *X—The Unknown* (1957) had a minor female character sent into shrieking fits by watching an intern melting into a grisly skeleton.

It wasn't until the company's first color horror feature, *The Curse of Frankenstein* (1957) that Hammer's Scream Queen image began to take shape into the form and look that has been referred to by some Hammer historians and devotees as Hammer Glamour. The distinction of being the company's first Scream Queens go to Hazel Court and Valerie Gaunt, who played characters of totally opposite types. Court (who had been in the business since 1944 at age 17) was cast as Baron Frankenstein's, aka Peter Cushing's, fiancée, Elizabeth. Unwilling to believe that her intended was up to monstrous doings in that locked room in Frankenstein manor, she fit the stereotyped genre heroine. Court was attractive, trusting and unwilling to believe the worst of the man she loved. Her character also

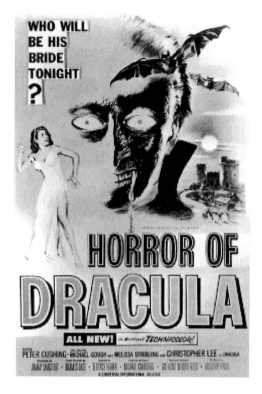

WHO WILL BE HIS BRIDE TONIGHT?

HORROR OF DRACULA

ALL NEW! *in gorgeous* TECHNICOLOR!

PETER CUSHING · MICHAEL GOUGH *and* MELISSA STRIBLING *and* CHRISTOPHER LEE *as* DRACULA

favored demure dress. Even nightgowns or robes were proper enough to fit that image—but still designed to catch male viewers' attention. Valerie Gaunt, on the other hand, made a full-color impact on male audiences as the film's nominal bad girl, Justine, the Frankenstein maid, who was carrying on a hot-and-heavy affair with her master and wearing (for the '50s) sexy nightgowns and robes. Not to mention some Eastmancolor cleavage (or Warner Color if you saw the film in America). Of course you knew she would come to a bad end; tradition demanded it! Plus she was pregnant by the Baron and was going to throw a monkey wrench into his intended nuptials. One guess who was destined to become a victim of Frankenstein's Monster (Christopher Lee).

Beside the obvious first of this color Frankenstein film, you can see that *The Curse of Frankenstein* featured more than just a casual nod to sex as part of the plot. But this was only a warm-up for what was to come next.

Horror of Dracula [original title in Britain: *Dracula*] (1958) not only took the vampire movie genre and shook it until its fangs rattled, but it also had more of a sexual aspect thanks to Christopher Lee's Count Dracula. who gave vampires of the past a run for their money when it came to claiming his attractive victims in their boudoir. (That's bedroom to you.)

Valerie Gaunt returned for her second Hammer appearance as The Vampire Woman (no name, just The Vampire Woman or Dracula's Bride) in a sequence that is one of the film's memorable moments, begging vampire hunter Jonathan Harker (John Van Eyssen) for help in escaping the Count, crying, then giving in to her undead bloodlust and going in

Valerie Gaunt and John Van Eyssen in *Horror of Dracula*

for the bite…er, kill. Any male member of the audience over the age of puberty had to be bowled over by the sight of Gaunt in her Grecian style dress and cleavage that made her a vampire woman who embodied the slogan "so round, so firm, so fully packed." Of course, the sequences where Dracula claims Lucy (Carol Marsh) and Mina (Melissa Stribling) had their impact, but they never quite had the effect that Valerie Gaunt's moment on screen had. The lasting memory of that sequence was saluted over 40 years later by Jim Wynorski in his horror spoof *Transylvania Twist* in a scene where he virtually recreated, almost shot for shot, this moment, with Monique Gabrielle taking over as the well-rounded vampire.

However, cleavage was not a major aspect of the Hammer females. For the most part, with certain exceptions, the heroines who appeared in Hammer's productions were usually demure in their behavior (if they were the good girls; and sometimes they even gave the bad girls some competition when they went after something or somebody they really wanted) and well clothed. If they appeared in nightgowns, the outfits were comparatively proper, yet such moments were looked forward to by the male contingent of the audience.

Attack of the B Queens   89

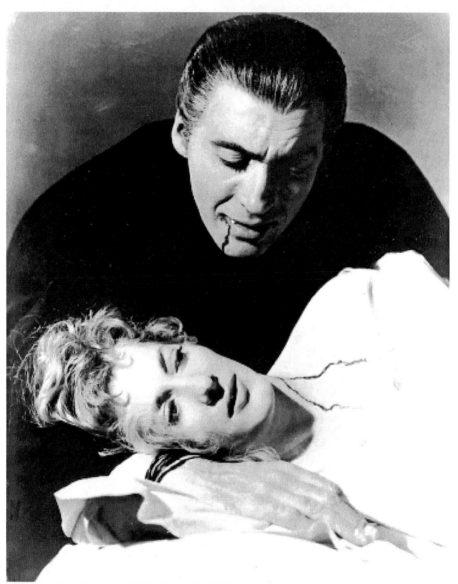

Christopher Lee and Melissa Stribling in a seductive publicity shot for
Horror of Dracula

In selecting the female leads for their post-*Curse of Frankenstein*
productions, Hammer discovered actresses who were not only attractive
but were ideal for the publicity campaigns that followed. Needless to
say, this always helped increase the fan's anticipation of each new film.
Especially since in those days there were no magazines dedicated spe-
cifically to the horror heroines as we have today (*Scream Queens Illus-*

Yvonne Furneaux and Christopher Lee in _The Mummy_

trated, Femme Fatales, etc.). When you came right down to it, exploitation and promotion were the name of the game. In other words, good old-fashioned showmanship. And Hammer's chief, Sir James Carreras, was a master at promotion. Hammer historian Keith Dudley summarized the Hammer discoveries quite accurately when he declared, "...the female leads were always gorgeous, busty and nine times out of 10 foreign!"

Well, not quite nine out of 10 of Hammer's leading actresses were foreign, but the continental aspect of the late 1950s/early 1960s Hammer ladies added to the enjoyment of a Hammer production (although most of the ladies only made one, or in rare cases two, Hammer appearances). Marla Landi was earthy and, in the end, downright deadly in 1959's _The Hound of the Baskervilles_, while Yvonne Furneaux, in her only Hammer appearance, did double duty as Princess Ananka and future look-alike Isobel Banning in _The Mummy_ (1959). Lillian Brousse

Yvonne Monlaur and David Peel in *The Brides of Dracula*

raised male temperatures while Oliver Reed went *Paranoiac* (1964) and exotic Jeanne Roland, despite having her voice re-dubbed for *Curse of the Mummy's Tomb* (1964), was attractive Mummy fodder (with an exotic belly dancer thrown in as a bonus). Fashion model Carita was the title sword-wielding lead in *The Viking Queen* (1967) while Czech actress Olinka Berova was brought in to take the place of Ursula Andress in *The Vengeance of She* (1967). Neither discovery made an impact with Hammer fans. In Berova's case, while she was very pleasing on the male eyes, she did not have the impact of Andress (to whom she bore a minor resemblance).

Yvonne Monlaur, promoted by Hammer's publicity department as "France's latest sex kitten…" was very fetching vampire bait for David Peel's Baron Meinster in *The Brides of Dracula* (1960), considered to be one of Hammer's all-time best. After nearly becoming dinner for the Undead, she added to the exotic atmosphere of *Terror of the Tongs* (1960) as a fetching Tong slave in a tight-fitting outfit.

However, what some Hammer fans recall was the cleavage that, as time wore on, would sometimes become more and more prominent. One year after Valerie Gaunt raised temperatures in *Horror of Dracula*, Marie Devereaux sent male hormones into cyclotron-speed activity in *The Stranglers of Bombay* (1959), a costume thriller dealing with the Thuggee stranglers of India during the 19th century. Even without any dialogue, Devereaux's Thuggee maiden, Karim, caused the French movie critic M. Caine to declare (or more accurately drooled it as described in the remarkable book *The Hammer Story*) that Marie's "stunningly exposed bosom is of quite demential sumptuousness..." In Hammer's publicity for the film, Marie was called "the girl with the exuberant statistics!" Little wonder that the lady in the wide-cleavage costume was one of the attractions that caught male viewers by the (ahem) throat. Once again, it was the bad girl of the film who paved the way for cleavage.

Yvonne Romain in a publicity shot for *The Curse of the Werewolf*

Yvonne Romaine would be the next possessor of such exuberant statistics in two period chillers, *The Curse of the Werewolf* (1960) and *Night Creatures* [origingal title, *Captain Clegg*] (1961). Unlike Marie Devereux's character in *Stranglers*, Yvonne's exotic good looks and attention-catching proportion did not belong to a bad girl (she was a mute

Ursula Andress and John Richardson in *She*

put-upon servant girl in *Werewolf* and the innocent, unsuspecting daughter of a reformed pirate in *Creatures*), but the fans didn't care. She would get a chance to see how the other half lived in the costume drama *The Brigand of Kandahar* (1965) as the scheming sister to rebel leader Oliver Reed.

At this time, Hammer's already-established reputation for attractive female leads was given a major shot in the arm by two ladies who would only appear for the company once.

The first would be Ursula Andress who co-starred with Peter Cushing and Christopher Lee in Hammer's adaptation of H. Rider Haggard's classic adventure-fantasy, *She* (1965). In magnificent costumes, Andress gave audiences a memorable physical presence as the centuries-old Ayesha. aka She Who Must Be Obeyed.

The second was Raquel Welch, who became the pin-up favorite of millions via her fur-and-doeskin bikini role in *One Million Years B.C.* Welch was more of a reluctant Hammer performer having been cast in the film as a result of a production deal between Hammer and 20th Century Fox. Sure that nobody would really remember the film ("I can shove it under the carpet," she is quoted as having thought), Welch soon learned differently upon the film's release. Years later, it is still one of the films she is remembered for. The film's success also resulted in three more

Christopher Lee and Barbara Shelley in *Rasputin—The Mad Monk*

prehistoric world costumers: *Slave Girls*, aka *Prehistoric Women* (1968), *When Dinosaurs Ruled the Earth* (1970) and *Creatures the World Forgot* (1971), each one containing *One Million Years'* tradition of scantily clad cave girl beauties.

However, among the large number of actresses that graced Hammer's productions, there are certain performers who have become synonymous with Hammer Films.

After Hazel Court, Barbara Shelley could truly be considered Hammer's next Scream Queen, making her first appearance in *Shadow of the Cat* (1961), a little-seen gothic thriller co-produced with BHP Films.

Suzan Farmer and Barbara Shelley in *Dracula—Prince of Darkness*

In the chilling *The Gorgon* (1964) she was a tormented heroine who unwittingly housed the soul of the mythical horror, turning at least three people to stone during the chilling proceedings. In 1965, she found herself doing double duty on two features shot virtually back to back, *Dracula—Prince of Darkness* and *Rasputin—The Mad Monk* (both released in 1966). In *Rasputin*, she played one of the members of the Russian Court whom Rasputin uses, seduces and then discards when she realizes the truth about the hypnotic monk (Christopher Lee). *Dracula*, however, saw her start out as an overly prim and almost shrewish member of a party of four traveling through the Carpathians. Before the film was over she had succumbed to vampire Christopher Lee's bite and became a sensual bloodlusting member of the Undead, zeroing in on her attractive sister-in-law (Suzan Farmer) with a bit of lustful intention. Her final appearance for Hammer was in one of the company's best, *Quatermass and the Pit* [*5 Million Years to Earth* in the U.S.] (1967) as paleontologist Barbara Judd who is one of those possessed by the Martian version of the wild hunt. In all, Barbara Shelley appeared in seven films for Hammer (including their two brutal WW II dramas, *The Camp*

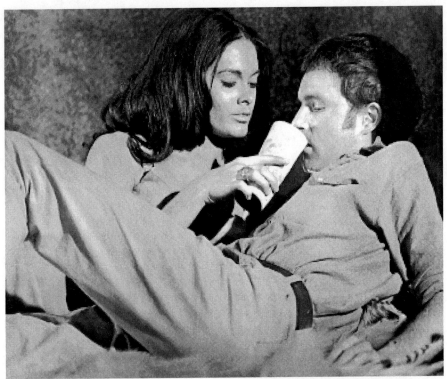

Martine Beswicke and Michael Latimer in _Prehistoric Women_

on Blood Island and _The Secret of Blood Island_), a starring record that has not been equaled in Hammer's history.

Even though Raquel Welch received top billing in the cast of _One Million Years, B.C._, Martine Beswicke gave her some stiff competition, capturing a good share of the male audience's attention as the jealous Nupondi. While Welch projected a sweet, albeit sexy, innocence in her skimpy prehistoric outfit, the pantherish Beswicke, in a skimpy but not as elegant animal skin costume, broadcast a feral animal magnetism that caused producer/director Michael Carreras to cast her as the lead in _Slave Girls/Prehistoric Women_ the following year. Despite a ridiculous script that probably made it difficult for the cast to keep a straight face at times, Beswicke dominated the picture, stalking about in her symbols of tribe leadership, cracking the whip on slave girls or the male she intended to have for her own, and generally leaving her marks on the studio scenery. Produced in 1966, the film was not released until two years later. Her last and most memorable role for Hammer was as the best-looking alter-ego for Robert Louis Stevenson's Dr. Henry Jekyll. _Dr. Jekyll and Sister_

Martine Beswicke seduces another victim in *Dr. Jekyll and Sister Hyde*.

Hyde (1971) had Beswicke in the role that is remembered best by many Hammer fans, the homicidal result of Dr. Jekyll's legendary personality-changing potion. As it came during the period when some of Hammer's productions were upping the skin quotient for their female leads, it gave audiences some memorable views of Beswicke's physical charms as she gave a magnificent portrayal of the dominating will to survive and evil of Sister Hyde.

Even though she only appeared in three Hammer productions, Veronica Carlson has remained a steadfast favorite with Hammer fans by radiating a combination of innocence and sexiness—a perfect Hammer heroine. Veronica became the object of Christopher Lee's evil intentions In *Dracula Has Risen from the Grave* (1968). But it was in *Frankenstein Must Be Destroyed* (1969) that she was really put through the mill as the Baron Frankenstein-tormented Anna Spengler, giving a magnificent performance as a victim driven to a full-scale breakdown. One of her most memorable moments occurs when a water main bursts, threatening to unearth a corpse buried in the backyard. Guess who has to get

Veronica Carlson and Barry Andrews in *Dracula Has Risen from the Grave*

the body hidden again without anyone's help (well, she couldn't ask for help...I mean, what would the neighbors think?). The following year, Veronica Carlson made her last Hammer appearance in *The Horror of Frankenstein* (1970), a remake of *The Curse of Frankenstein*, but with an attempt at dark humor. This time she was cast in Hazel Court's role of the Baron's fiancée, Elizabeth, still unaware of what her fiancé is up to both in creating a Monster and having it off with the housekeeper (Kate O'Mara). Veronica Carlson had that special something that, combined with her acting talent, made her one of the permanent favorites of Hammer Films around the world.

With *The Vampire Lovers* (1970), Hammer pushed the horror envelope and gave audiences a vampire movie that gave a new twist to the mythos, bringing it a little closer to the modern Scream Queen concept, namely showing more skin. At least in the case of some of the female cast members. Co-produced by American-International, based on Sheridan Le Fanu's story *Carmilla,* the film starred Polish-born Ingrid Pitt, who had been seen by James Carreras in *Where Eagles Dare.* As the undead Carmilla Karnstein, Pitt's vampire did more than just sink her

Carmilla (Ingrid Pitt) attacks the governess (Kate O'Mara) when she protests Carmilla's infatuation with Emma in *The Vampire Lovers*.

fangs into her victims' jugulars. She wooed them, actually falling in love with them during the process of their entrapment. Then, after they passed away, she moved on to fresher targets. Pitt not only hit home with fans with the same impact as a vampire's bite, but she embodied an aspect of the vampire that had only been hinted at in previous Hammer Films, the bisexual aspect of the Undead. In Carmilla's case, she displayed a preference for members of her own sex, but was more than willing to do in a male donor. As if this wasn't enough, *The Vampire Lovers* presented the first topless female vampire and victim in the persons of the exotic Pitt and doe-eyed, slender and also busty Madeline Smith (who had made her first appearance in a Hammer film as an innocent-looking prostitute in *Taste the Blood of Dracula* the year before and would deliver an effective performance as the mute Sarah in *Frankenstein and the Monster From Hell* (1972)). As an added plus, Kate O'Mara was cast as Smith's

INGRID PITT: VAMPIRE LOVERS
In Her Own Words

Hammer started, for me, at the Grosvenor Hotel in December 1969. It was at the height of my Premiere Queen days. A polite way of saying I was "between films," a euphemism for out of work. *Alfred the Great* had just premiered at the Odeon in Leicester Square, London, and everyone had moved on to the hotel for dinner and congratulations. I found myself sitting next to a military-looking gent who spent most of the evening shaking hands with anyone who sidled up to the table and touched a forelock. When things simmered down a bit he introduced himself. James Carreras. I dimpled prettily and said I was pleased to meet him. He complimented me on my last film–*Where Eagles Dare*. I let him enthuse. He also asked me what I was doing next. Number one rule of a resting thespian is never admit you haven't got a raft of producers just begging to put you in front of their camera. James nodded and I had the distinct impression he had heard it all before. He introduced me to his wife and for the rest of the evening we went through the same old formula of brightly inane conversation followed by awkward silences. When it was time to go I met Mr. Carreras again in the foyer. He offered me his card and suggested that I come to see him the following morning at his office in Wardour Street—he might have three roles for me. I disguised my feelings well. I thought it was a try on. At that time I was getting a lot of interest from producers. Usually an invitation back to their hotel room to discuss a script. Which usually led to the suggestion of a run through on the bed. And me a respectable girl! Next morning, after a restless night, I decided that the appointment was in his office and as I had nothing else planned I might as well go along.

In spite of my initial trepidation I braved the wind and slush of a November morn in 1969 to audition for the part. I decked myself out in the shortest micro skirt, little more than a wide belt, thigh-length boots, a flowing maxi-coat and topped it off with a wide brimmed Fedora. Jimmy sat behind his desk. I waited until I had his full attention then shrugged off the coat to reveal the skirt and breath-restricting sweater. I let the coat fall onto the settee and whipped off the hat and let my golden tresses speak for themselves. I perched a buttock on the arm of the sofa, smiled brightly and said something cringe-making like "Private Pitt reporting for duty, Colonel." I'll give him his due, he didn't laugh. Just nodded politely. "I've got a film called *Vampire Lovers* starting in January. I think you'd be just right for the lead," he said in an offhand manner.

Within a very few weeks I was picked up in a limo and driven to Elstree to start work on *Vampire Lovers*. A bit like the Hokey-Pokey! You put your left leg in, you put your left leg out, turn around—and that's what it's all about.

Ingrid Pitt as the real-life Elizabeth Bathory in *Countess Dracula*

governess who was also attracted to Pitt's vampire. The combination of Hammer's almost-patented Gothic horror, more than a touch of lesbianism and tits and fangs made *The Vampire Lovers* one of Hammer's hits for the year. It also spawned two sequels (*Lust for a Vampire* and *Twins of Evil*), with the overall group referred to as the Karnstein trilogy.

Pitt would appear once more for the company in *Countess Dracula* (1971). But instead of a member of the Undead, she portrayed a real-life blood-thirster, the notorious bloody countess Elizabeth Bathory, who killed young girls so she could bathe in their virgin blood, and therefore remain young and beautiful. As the youth-obsessed Countess, Pitt starts out as an old woman, becomes young and beautiful and then goes on killing to keep that beauty. Ingrid Pitt threw herself into the role and when she wasn't wearing gorgeous period costumes, gave audiences a moment or two of her au naturel self. Although her film appearances have been few, she is still one of those actresses who is identified with Hammer.

The more liberal policy of bare skin continued in the sequel to *Vampire Lovers*, *Lust for a Vampire* (1971) with Yutte Stensgaard making her only Hammer appearance as the vampiric Carmilla, stalking her victims at a girls' boarding school. The same year saw Mary and Madelaine Collinson (who had gained fame as *Playboy*'s first-ever twin playmates

Twins of Evil was the final entry in the Karnstein saga.

in 1970) as _Twins of Evil_, the finale to the Karnstein saga. Actually, only one of the twins was evil, Frieda, played by Madelaine. She becomes involved with the villainous Count Karnstein who becomes vampirized by the spirit of his ancestor Carmilla/Mircalla. He in turn puts the bite on Frieda who proceeds to raise hell and almost gets her sister burned at the stake by fanatic Puritans, led by Peter Cushing.

Caroline Munro made only two appearances for Hammer. In _Dracula A.D. 1972_ she was one of a group of mod teenagers (along with future star Stephanie Beacham), who unwittingly helped resurrect Christopher Lee's Dracula, and, as a reward, was the first to get drained by the vampire. Her second appearance was in _Captain Kronos Vampire Hunter_ (1972—released in 1974), an attempt to mix the swashbuckler and the vampire together. Munro played Carla, a Gypsy who winds up journeying with the title character (Horst Janson) and his partner Prof. Grost (John Cater) to get to the bottom of some unusual vampire killings. Munro projected a certain sensuality (which had stood her in good stead as a model who was the main attraction of a series of billboards advertising

Valerie Leon made a memorable appearance in *Blood from the Mummy's Tomb*.

Lamb's, Navy Rum) that made her a fan favorite. Roles in such non-Hammer films as *Golden Voyage of Sinbad* and *At the Earth's Core* and the James Bond thriller *The Spy Who Loved Me* confirmed her allure and talent.

Statuesque (5' 11") Valerie Leon made one memorable appearance for Hammer in the troubled production *Blood from the Mummy's Tomb* (1971). As the look-alike of an ancient Egyptian queen named Tera, who just happened to be an evil sorceress, Leon became the target of plans to resurrect the evil sorceress. It would have been interesting to see what further use Hammer would have made of her if fate had been different.

Julie Ege joined the lineup of skin-bikini-clad heroines in *Creatures the World Forgot* (1971), a so-so windup to Hammer's prehistoric world pictures, with the curvy Miss Ege being one of the few memorable aspects. She returned to Hammer two years later, wearing a bit more clothing, for the studio's co-production of *The Legend of the Seven Golden Vampires* (1974) with Hong Kong's Shaw Brothers. While her obvious

Caroline Munro, Stephanie Beacham, Marsha Hunt and Janet Key with Christopher Lee for a promo shot for *Dracula A.D., 1972*

charms were hidden...somewhat...she got a chance to be an attractive vampire in the film's ending, making it one of the rare times that a Hammer heroine didn't survive to the fade-out.

In the company's last theatrical chiller, a Scream Queen turned up again in *To the Devil a Daughter* (1976) when a nude Nastassja Kinski appeared before occult authority Richard Widmark, courtesy of devil-worshipping minister Christopher Lee.

There have been others who have appeared in Hammer's productions, but these were the ones who are either most identified with the company's films or seemed to fit into the still-developing image of the Scream Queen. In 1972, Hammer producer/director Michael Carreras said, "A Hammer girl is someone who is very pleasing to look at for 90 minutes...and who you would like to see more of after that." Hammer excelled in that respect, and it was these actresses who left the fans wanting more.

THE ART OF SCREAMING:
The 1980s
by Brinke Stevens

It was somewhere in Hollywood, circa 1981, that I first sat in Roger Corman's office at New World Pictures. Clutched in my hand was a battered copy of *Dramalog* magazine, where I'd hastily circled an "Actors Wanted" advertisement: "A dozen pretty young girls are needed to get naked and die horribly." Maybe it was the way I screamed so convincingly at that audition, or perhaps the fact that I agreed to bare my breasts and get covered in bloody goo. That fateful day, I was cast in *Slumber Party Massacre* to play a hapless teenage victim of an escaped homicidal maniac.

Although I realized it was just another low-budget knife-kill flick, I was so thrilled to get that lead part. After I moved to Los Angeles the year prior, I'd mainly supported myself by background extra jobs, music videos (back when MTV still played them) and a few modeling assignments. Now, I got my very first speaking role and it also was the first time I took a cinematic shower, screamed loudly and was brutally slain on the big screen.

Little did I know that my own film career would prove to be a perfect paradigm for the whole phenomenon of 1980s B-grade horror movies. It seems every film decade has had its own unique character—and the '80s were off the charts in terms of innovative splatter scenarios, high body counts and lots of gratuitous nudity.

Although *Slumber Party Massacre* was my original launch into future B-movie fame, it was, admittedly, rather derivative. It echoed *The Driller Killer* (1979), by featuring a maniac at large with an electric drill who terrorizes an all-girl slumber party. Despite the voyeuristic shower scene and a dozen gutted female victims, three of the girls ultimately team up to thwart the murderous psychopath. To its credit, it was later considered to be the first feminist exploitation film. Penned by novelist Rita Mae Brown and directed by Amy Jones, fresh from film school at MIT, it paved the way for strong female heroines later in the decade.

So saying, *Slumber Party Massacre* (1982) was yet another offering into the new slasher subgenre that flooded drive-in screens, so popular from 1978 to 1984. As a spin-off of the mature psycho-thriller genre, it pointedly catered to a booming youth market by a pat formula: a conspicuous absence of adults, sexually active teenagers, a seemingly indestructible killer and gory murders.

I suspect the genre illustriously began back in 1974, with Tobe Hooper's *Texas Chain Saw Massacre*. Though pre-dated by *Psycho* (1960), it was possibly the first true slasher film and set the trend for the late 1970s and early '80s. It was based on the actual story of Ed Gein, a handyman in Wisconsin, who liked to dig up fresh graves and then skin the corpses to wear upon his own body. When I first saw it in a theater, I was utterly numb with shock. Though cheaply shot, it was intense, crazed and relentless enough to soon become a major cult classic.

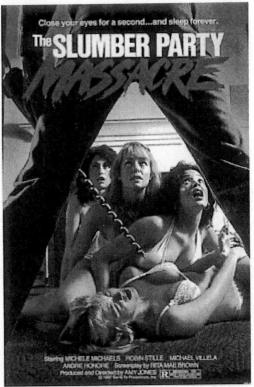

As a true horror aficionado, I watched a new cycle start in 1978 with John Carpenter's *Halloween*. Again, it furthered the human monster motif and it, too, was considered responsible for the early 1980s stalk-'n'-slash trend. But as horror writer-director Jason Collum so succinctly states:

> It took what was considered the last safe place in America—suburbia—and turned it into a place of death and horror. It was also the first film in which a human villain—shot, stabbed and sent falling from a second-story balcony—was unstoppable and got away in the end, a trend almost every horror film has used since.

Although *Halloween* was completed in only 20 days on a tight $300,000 budget, it would soon change the face of the genre forever. Many consider it to be the father of slasher films, although it showed surprisingly little graphic violence and almost no gore. An important element of *Halloween*'s success was our ability to identify with the trio of female protagonists. In the beginning, a grade-school aged Michael Myers kills his promiscuous sister with a butcher knife, and later only the virginal protagonist (Jamie Lee Curtis) survives. "Ever since *Halloween*," claims critic James Berardinelli, "the standard for slasher films has been that sexual promiscuity leads to a violent end."

Soon after *Halloween*'s 1978 release, critics began to notice that it offered more than initially met the eye. For one thing, it took advantage of the very obvious, neglected fact that the most horrific night of the year had never been used in a horror movie. Thus, it launched a new holiday-horror trend that was soon seized upon by the *Friday the 13th* series, plus a string of Christmas-themed offerings: *You Better Watch Out* (1980), *To All a Goodnight* (1983), *Don't Open Till Christmas* (1984), and *Silent Night, Deadly Night* (1984).

I'd also say that it originated more than a few of today's common horror movie clichés. As Berardinelli explains:

> It didn't take long for someone to decide that audiences wanted as many explicitly grisly scenes as the running length would allow. By the time *Halloween*'s sequel was released in 1981, the objective of this sort of movie was no longer to scare its viewers, but to gross them out.

It encouraged an onslaught of other imitation films: *When a Stranger Calls* (1979), *Don't Go in the House* (1980), *He Knows You're Alone* (1980), *Prom Night* (1980), *The Boogeyman* (1980), *Graduation Day* (1981), *Happy Birthday to Me* (1981), *Alone in the Dark* (1982) and many more.

While *Halloween* created a contemporary cycle of teenage jeopardy pictures, it was Sean Cunningham's *Friday the 13th* (1980) that capitalized on the maniac-on-the-loose trend and brought gore to mainstream America. It was the first slasher film to be picked up by a major studio, Paramount. Again, this cautionary tale featured nitwit teens and promiscuous camp counselors who are quickly sliced and diced by hockey-mask wearing Jason Voorhees, following in his murderous mother's footsteps...and it's up to the only virgin to save the day.

As slasher films started to lag in popularity, a fresh teens in terror film was produced in 1984—Wes Craven's *Nightmare on Elm Street*. Critics called it one of the most inventive and literate slasher films of the fabled 1980s. It featured Heather Langenkamp as a determined, resourceful heroine. But more importantly, it introduced Freddy Krueger (Robert Englund) as the villain, a truly frightening presence who was permanently burned in our imaginations. With his scarred face, battered fedora, grungy red-and-green striped sweater, and that glove with the six-inch blades, Freddy was quickly elevated to the movie-monster pantheon (aided by sequels, comic books, masks and other merchandise).

Jason Collum notes:

> It saved a dying genre from suffocation of slasher movie overload. As its sequels gained popularity, it created an entirely new subgenre—the dream/nightmare killer. It

also introduced the most famous horror icon of the last 25 years of the century and was also possibly *the* scariest movie of the decade. It was one of two films [*Friday the 13th* being the other one] to define '80s horror.

FRIDAY THE 13TH PART VIII
JASON TAKES MANHATTAN
COMING SOON

In fact, all the aforementioned movies spurred a huge trend for film sequels: *Texas Chain Saw Massacre* is now facing its fifth incarnation; *Halloween* has racked up nine so far; *Friday the 13th* spawned 10 by 2002; and *Nightmare on Elm Street* generated six spin-offs by 1994. It proved to Hollywood that sequels, no matter how good or lousy, could turn a profit.

Similar to Universal Studios' horror franchises in the 1930s, even the most marginally successful films of the early '80s sent low-budget companies clamoring for recognizable titles. Horror filmmakers went after brand names (like Michael, Jason, and Freddy) to sell their products, and sequels seemed almost the law for money-minded producers throughout the 1980s decade.

Believe me, I tried to stake my claim when I heard *Slumber Party Massacre* Parts 2 & 3 were being produced a few years later. All they said was, "But Brinke...you're already *dead!*" Hah! No imagination, honestly.

Scholar John F. Crossen laments:

> There are no more horror stars like Lugosi, Karloff, Price, and so on; only horror characters. Horror films become franchises. Sequel after sequel is what it's all about, not for personality sake or even art, but for pure profit. Even Norman Bates gets in on the act, with *Psycho* coming

Sissy Spacek as *Carrie*

back for three more rounds. The "Me Generation" finds
its counterpart in the horror genre: horror as unleashed
consumerism.

This hunger for consumerism gave us two celebrated stars who
brought lots of bloody mayhem and ghoulish laughter to the genre: prolific author Stephen King and horror hostess Elvira, Mistress of the Dark.

Stephen King burst onto the screen with telekinetic fury through the
success of 1976's horror classic *Carrie*. Although it was his first pub-
lished novel, King's sensitive storyline merged with Brian DePalma's
stylish direction to create a lonely, abused teenage character to whom

audiences could easily relate. When the movie became one of MGM's biggest hits, Stephen King quickly became horror's biggest author.

After a much-anticipated film version of *Salem's Lot* (1979), the early '80s saw the "King subgenre" take firm hold of the marketplace. Within the next few years, audiences were fed the supernatural fears of *The Shining* (1980), *Creepshow* (1982), *Dead Zone* (1983), *Cujo* (1983), *Children of the Corn* (1984) and *Firestarter* (1984). In 1989, *Pet Sematary* proved to be one of the most successful films of the decade, with a box office take nearing the $100 million mark. This furthered the trend into the early '90s, as yet more King novels were churned into movies: *Misery* (1990), *Graveyard Shift* (1990), *Dolores Clairborne* (1995) and many others. King, however, wasn't the only star of screams to emerge from '80s self-promotion and consumerism. It would seem he had a curvy cousin...

When Elvira, Mistress of the Dark, premiered on a Los Angeles tele-

Cassandra Peterson's Elvira

vision station in 1981 as a hostess of midnight schlock, the world wasn't quite yet aware of what she had in store for them. Embodied by a red-haired beauty named Cassandra Peterson, Elvira soon became the vamp of horror.

With her black beehive hairdo, striking makeup, and prominent cleavage bursting out of her barely legal dress, she was a self-confessed "purveyor of pulchritude." Sort of a successor to Carolyn Jones' Morticia Addams, Yvonne de Carlo's Lily Munster, and the pioneering horror hostess Vampira, Elvira gleefully cracked "boobs and butts" jokes which made her an immediate hit with teenage boys. As her TV show *Movie Macabre* became a nationwide hit, so did Elvira.

Luckily, her counterpart was a slick and savvy businesswoman. Peterson quickly realized her assets were quite valuable and began promoting herself into the industry's best-known female icon (after buying the rights to her character). Her popularity exploded in the late 1980s, leading to her own full-length feature, 1988's hilarious self-titled horror-comedy, *Elvira, Mistress of the Dark*, which epitomized everything Elvira had come to stand for.

As Jason Paul Collum relates:

> Elvira is essentially the horror fan's Marilyn Monroe. She's worshipped by women for her strength and humor, by straight men for her plunging neckline, and by gay men for her presence. She's made herself into an industry, a feat few other actresses of any genre have accomplished.

The early '80s was quite an exciting time for devout genre fanciers like myself. You could still see nearly every horror release on the big screen, complete and uncut. The gore was exceedingly graphic, as dismembered corpses piled up. There was a sadistic, voyeuristic sexism; a sense of cruelty and uncanny menace; a succession of low-budget visual atrocities: throats cut, spears through guts, limbs lopped off, brains splattered, and eyes gouged out. Chainsaws, machetes, power drills, axes, and nail guns were the weapons of choice in these dark, often shocking horror flicks.

By the '90s, I'd say I was killed in nearly every possible cinematic way: skewered by an electric drill, throat slit by a razor blade, shot with guns and arrows, sliced by a scythe, blown up by a hand grenade in my mouth, pulled apart by demons, and so on. *Well, hey, it's a living....*

HAVE A FUN-FILLED
VACATION!
Toe-Tapping
Machete Head Dances!
Glamourous Zombie-Style
Cosmetic Surgery!
Fabulous
Air-Conditioned
Tiger Pits!

Zombie
Island
Massacre

DAVID BROADNAX • RITA JENRETTE

As such, *Friday the 13th* carved yet another notch, when it became the main target of the watchdog force of the MPAA (a movie ratings board). Thanks to the stunningly bloody make-up effects of wizard Tom Savini, it spurred two well-known film critics (Siskel and Ebert) to begin their war on stalker films, which led to the MPAA's crackdown on violence and gore for theatrical releases. Much like the 1950s, horror films in the '80s became controversial and hotly debated, largely for their purely exploitative content.

As theatrical releases began losing their power with a crusading MPAA on their tails, the genre's next big boost came with the increasing popularity of direct-to-video releases around 1985. Practically overnight, a whole new market for the horror industry reared its head. At that point, any film ever produced had only one option: to play in a movie theater. Gradually, as huge conglomerate chains built multiplexes in shopping malls, the many small drive-ins and art house theaters were eradicated, thus severely restricting the formerly wide variety of fare for a public audience.

Almost in response to a dying plea, a new option arose in the boom of home video technology. By 1979, it's estimated that only 10,000 VCRs existed in households across America. Yet by mid-decade, over 27,000 new mom & pop video stores suddenly sprang up in our neighborhoods, and they all had lots of empty shelves to fill with new direct-

Attack of the B Queens

to-video products. Those trendy films were made by people who once made, or, in the case of the younger generation, would have made, theatrical features.

Unlike major film distribution companies, which had become ever more selective about products they released (due to the high cost of marketing), enterprising filmmakers found that you could produce just about anything on video and laugh all the way to the bank.

As Anthony Timpone (editor of *Fangoria*), so aptly stated:

> Many independent producers bypassed theatrical distribution and went right into the living room, giving birth to the direct-to-video phenomenon. The shelves at local video stores were overflowing with terror titles, many unrated...video became the last holdout for unrated, uncensored splatter. Every independent producer in Hollywood with the least bit of clout jumped on the slasher bandwagon.

Partially, I rather agree with writer Steve Perry, who insists:

> The problem with this century is that with the rise of the individual, standards have fallen really low since everything is subjective. That's why we're awash in trash.

Yet John McCarthy refutes, in his excellent book *The Sleaze Merchants* (1995):

> It's easy—but not at all fair—just to dismiss the work of the sleaze merchants as "trash" aimed at the "lowest common denominator" of the movie-going public, and therefore not worth preserving, let alone writing about. Working on paltry budgets, yet competing for the same customer's hard-earned buck, they had to be shrewd showmen first and foremost. They had to be able to smell a trend, or seize on a subject heretofore untouched by Hollywood. Then they had to be fast on their feet in exploiting that trend, by shooting their films and rushing them into distribution with almost lightning speed.

"Casting agents sent me out for small background parts..."

Obviously, nudity and gore were two key exploitable trends of home video products...which spontaneously created their own traditions, stars and fans. In low-budget films, there really didn't seem to be an option for baring one's flesh; they emphasized that right up front. As Joe Bob Briggs pointed out, "beasts, babes and blood" were the equation for success, and babes abruptly became a stunningly valuable commodity.

Reviewer Richard Corliss noted, "And everywhere, bosoms, so large and preternaturally firm, thanks to the miracle of plastic surgery. Cleavage has it all over big stunts and pricey morphing effects." Confirms director Fred Olen Ray, "Breasts are the cheapest special effect in our business." Producer Charles Band, head of Empire Pictures and later Full Moon, advises, "Make sure the ads feature sleazy drawings of lots of bosomy women, and a knife blade or two. If someone with a large bosom can be shown wielding a knife, so much the better. If you can throw in a spurting artery, better yet."

In the mid-1980s, many big-name actresses still shunned nudity as instant career death. Although the public clamored for it, a new need arose for body doubles and nude extras. Having no prudish hang-ups, I mostly paid my rent by appearing naked on screen. Since the going rate

Linnea Quigley

for a clothed actor was $35 a day, yet unclothed work netted $1,000, it was a logical choice for a young actress attempting to survive in Hollywood.

Casting agents sent me out for small background parts that required nudity, like shower or locker room scenes, soft-core bits for *The Playboy Channel*, or the occasional body double job (like for *Psycho 3*). I appeared in a few *Playboy* and *Penthouse* glamour layouts, too. In truth, it was my own willingness to bare my body that initially opened a huge door to B movie success (as evidenced by my earlier shower scene in *Slumber Party Massacre*). If I'd staunchly clung to my modesty, I certainly would not be where I am today as a cult celebrity.

In 1982, I first met my illustrious partners of future horror fame, Linnea Quigley and Michelle Bauer, when we showered together on the set of *The Man Who Wasn't There*. Statuesque, tanned and good-natured, Michelle had already appeared in a glut of men's magazines (including a *Penthouse* centerfold), all-girl fetish videos and soft-core adult films like *Café Flesh* (1982), often under the pseudonym of Pia Snow.

While she now demurely downplays her sexy past, saying "I just turned my mind off and went to work," she admits it all helped her to get recognized later on. Michelle's feelings about nudity: "My theory is that if YOU don't do it, honey, someone else will. If you go to a reading and nudity is required, are you going to walk out the door just when you're finally getting a break?"

Posing with Linnea and Michelle at Chiller Theatre convention

Michelle's breakthrough film was Fred Olen Ray's *The Tomb* in 1985, playing the lead role of a reincarnated Egyptian princess. It began an enduring partnership between the actress and producer, soon leading to her portrayal of a mute cave bunny in *Phantom Empire* (1986) and another bit in *Armed Response* (1986), continuing into the '90s with her nicely villainous turn in *Little Miss Magic*.

She muses, "Sometimes I see actresses in a big studio movie and I think, I could be doing that, no problem. But they also get a lot of crap along with the fame and money, so it's a trade-off. I just want to be financially comfortable and enjoy my work. When it stops being fun, then I'll walk."

Linnea Quigley, a petite blonde dynamo, arrived in Hollywood in 1976, following her high school graduation. She found work at a health spa and soon opted to model for men's magazines. "All I could think of to justify what I was doing," she explains, "was that this was just a career step. It was a way to make it into show business." In 1979, she landed a featured role in Charles Band's sex-farce *Fairy Tales*, as Sleeping Beauty.

"I found out that my character was supposed to have sex on camera," Linnea relates. "It's not that I'd led some sort of puritan existence up to that point, but I was rather shocked. How could I do something that private for the entertainment of everyone who'd see the movie?" She adds that the money she earned from such jobs kept her in the business. "That," she says, "and my continuing hope that eventually the movie offers would start coming in and I'd never have to pose naked for strangers again. At least I was half-right."

Her horror movie career took off like a rocket early in the decade. She did a topless scene in *Don't Go Near The Park* (1979), played a seductive bitch in *Summer Camp* (1979), succumbed as "victim #1" in *Stone Cold Dead* (1979), and got naked before dying in *Graduation Day* (1981). In her autobiography, *I'm Screaming As Fast As I Can* (1995), Quigley remarks:

> This was the beginning of the major theme in my career, playing the tart who dies in some hideous manner. I figured somebody had to do it, so it might as well be me. I was just glad to be getting the work, so long as none of that stuff was happening to me in real life. I suppose it

should have occurred to me that I was being typecast. I know that's death to some actors, but I was just having fun.

In 1984, Linnea suddenly found herself amidst a storm of controversy generated by *Silent Night, Deadly Night*, a slasher film in the Christmas subgenre. Naked and impaled on deer antlers, she was one of several Yule-themed murder victims. Jason Collum elaborates:

> Though the film itself was rather forgettable, TV ads during family hour created an uproar with parents and censorship groups. It quickly made a bundle at the box office, but was also quickly pulled from release to calm the protests.

It seems people resented the idea of portraying Santa Claus as a deranged serial killer. Nonetheless, it spawned four sequels by 1991.

The major film that finally put Linnea on the map was Dan O'Bannon's *Return of the Living Dead* (1985). Cast as a zombie punkette named Trash, she was required to do a seductive strip tease in a graveyard and then get devoured by carnivorous corpses. She wryly remarks, "After sitting uncomfortably on antlers, I thought I'd experienced the worst prop and make-up hell I could ever go through. I was wrong." As a zombie, she wore a "Barbie doll" appliance over her private parts and suffered a face mask glued to her skin for 12 hours a day for a week, while she wallowed in freezing cold mud and fake torrential rain, only to stagger home with strep throat as the sun came up each day. Despite her travails, it's the one movie that really launched her into B-movie stardom.

Actually, Linnea's *Return of the Living Dead* was only one of many zombie films of the decade. It was ground already covered by screenwriter John Russo's *Night of the Living Dead* (1968) and George A. Romero's *Dawn of the Dead* (1979), which was hailed by some critics as a brilliant analogy of our times, and condemned by others as a violent, pretentious time-waster. In any case, once zombies had become flesh-eaters on screen, all sorts of taboos were broken to make them even more frightening. It proved that even the deceased won't put up with abuse forever, and they simply refused to take death lying down.

Linnea in *Return of the Living Dead*

A spate of ghoulish movies dominated our screens in the 1980s: *Hard Rock Zombies* (1984) featured a reanimated band of longhairs; George Romero's *Day of the Dead* (1985) was full of ghastly visual puns in the EC comics spirit; two sequels to *Return of the Living Dead* (1987 and 1993) exemplified every settle-for-less attitude of late-1980s horror cinema; Stuart Gordon's *Re-Animator* (1985) made a cult star of Barbara Crampton; Wes Craven's *Deadly Friend* (1986) was formulaic but fea-

tured Kristy Swanson in a pre-Buffy role. And not to mention *Zombie High* (1987); *Zombie Nightmare* (1987); yet more slapstick zombie gore in *Dead Heat* (1988); a zombie-Western called *Ghost Town* (1988); and Troma's *Chopper Chicks in Zombie Town* (1989), an exploitation flick with a mild feminist twist.

Perhaps the ultimate remake was 1990's *Night of the Living Dead*, where audiences saw a vast change in the stereotypically helpless female in peril. Actress Patricia Tallman ended up in fatigues sporting an Uzi...and it seemed perfectly appropriate for the take-no-prisoners '90s.

Suddenly, a new phenomenon of female horror stars arose as direct-to-video titles boomed in the late-1980s. John F. Crossen notes:

> Finally, the '80s consumer horror spills over onto its biggest commodity: its female bodies. And those who know how best to market those bodies, its Scream Queens, create a new franchise: themselves. The body-obsessed horror of the splatter films raises up new celebrities like Linnea, Brinke and Michelle. Embracing the two dimensions of horror (women as victim and victimizer), they fuse them into lasting careers with no apologies.

As a trio, our first film was David DeCoteau's *Sorority Babes in the Slimeball Bowl-A-Rama* (1987). The plot was rather unique: a punk burglar and a group of sorority girls break into a bowling alley to steal a trophy, unwittingly unleashing a demon imp. As usual, most of the teenage characters end up screaming and dying horribly.

It was an exceedingly demanding location shoot at a real bowling alley near San Diego, CA. We'd start filming at 9 p.m. when the place closed, and would later fall into our hotel beds around 9 a.m. (It's so weird to eat breakfast at 4 o'clock in the afternoon!) Linnea suffered many bruises herself, and I dislocated my knee in one of the fight scenes. Despite the pain, I loved the whole experience, and I must say it generated a truly fine little film on a basement budget.

Jason Collum points out:

> Though the movie itself didn't alter the genre, its three female leads did. Linnea Quigley, Brinke Stevens and Michelle Bauer became '80s B-movie scream queens. This was a bonus for the direct-to-video industry, because any one of their names on the front of a box cover from 1987 to 1991 practically guaranteed high-volume sales, which was a continuing boost for the genre.

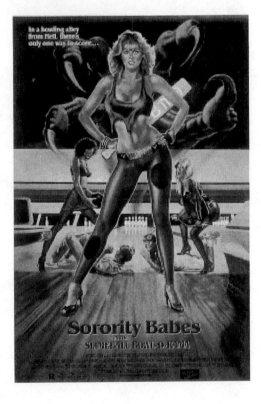

That same year, Linnea, Michelle and I teamed up a second time for DeCoteau's *Nightmare Sisters* (1987), working on an almost no-budget, four-day shooting schedule as nerdy college girls who turn into predatory hot babes after a sinister seance. Again, we three happily delivered precisely what our college-age male target audience wanted to see. In response, they enthusiastically turned us into cultural icons; rare female images among the male-dominated horror pantheon. Thanks to the high demand for new video products, we've each individually appeared in over 50 films to date.

With social progress, traditional female victim roles became a bit blurred in the late 1980s. Producer Fred Olen Ray nailed it, saying of his film *Biohazard* (1984):

Past, present and future scream queens: Adrienne Barbeau, Janet Leigh and Jamie Leigh Curtis with John Carpenter on the set of *The Fog*

It was then that we started giving female lead roles where they weren't required to die. We still killed women occasionally in the films, but it just seemed to me that people enjoyed seeing women do things other than cowering and shivering. The times had changed, and women weren't the sniveling, cowering creatures that we'd always pegged them to be.

John F. Crossen muses:

In horror literature or films, one thing seems certain—the need for a feminine presence, either as a damsel in distress or a wicked *femme fatale*. The actress may be called on to swoon into the arms of a mummy or swamp creature, or she herself becomes the monster. She may fill our celluloid memories with ear-piercing shrieks, or shudders at the shrieks she incited in others. The scream—particularly the female scream—is essential to horror films.

Fay Wray was probably the Queen Mother, emitting the most famous scream heard round the world in *King Kong* (1933). Crossen states that Fay Wray's screams were dubbed into other actresses' mouths well into the '40s.

Decades later, Jamie Lee Curtis debuted as possibly the first modern Scream Queen in *Halloween* (1978). Author Ted Newsom says, "Curtis came by the scream queen aspect of her career hereditarily: her mother, Janet Leigh, was memorably hacked to death in the shower of the Bates Motel in *Psycho* (1960)." After appearing in John Carpenter's *The Fog* (1980), *Terror Train* (1980), *Prom Night* (1980) and *Road Games* (1981), she capped her screaming phase with *Halloween II* (1981). Subsequently, Curtis blossomed into an actress of the first rank. Jamie Lee Curtis comments:

> To be the queen of genre females is an honor as long as you're intelligent about it. People have asked me to pose with a crown or a knife in my hand; that's the other extreme.

Critic Joe Bob Briggs reflects on *Texas Chain Saw Massacre*:

> Marilyn Burns, "The Screamer," is truly acknowledged to be the finest motion picture screamer known to mankind. But it might be because she had so much to scream about. It was 110 degrees inside the Cannibal House, and all the meat on the table was dead rotting animals filled with formaldehyde. Considering the smell, plus all the sticky blood they poured on Marilyn, plus the fact that she got dragged through the underbrush for a couple weeks and busted up both knees, you've got to figure those were real screams.

Actress Maria Ford, a willowy blonde who made 40 direct-to-video movies in eight years, said, "You have to *love* to act. The food is always bad, you never get any sleep, you work 17-hour days, the scripts change at the last minute." About nudity, she stated, "I'm willing to take off my clothes for 10% of a film so I can act in the other 90%."

Corman alumnus Starr Andreef, who was impregnated by a "man in a rubber suit" monster and killed herself in *The Terror Within* (1988), reflects, "My criterion for accepting a script was to ask, 'On what page do I die?' The longer you're alive, the more money you make." She still shudders to recall her vampire flick, *Dance of the Damned* (1988). "It was one of the hardest films I ever did: cuts, bruises, a scratched cornea. It was so mentally and physically exhausting to work 16 or 17 hour days for over three weeks, that afterwards I couldn't get out of bed for a month."

Scream Queens of the '80s, more so than our predecessors, rode that demanding crest of insane work and gory nudity. As Crossen puts it:

> With the phenomenal success of graphic horrors like *Friday the 13th*, we entered a bloody new age of top make-up effects, deformities, body wounds, and scripts that seemed to link the sex act with violent death...otherwise ticket sales would be anemic." Actress Teresa Lynn said of one of her films, "There's blood, blood, blood everywhere!...Did I mention there's blood?"

Michelle Bauer adds this about *Hollywood Chainsaw Hookers* (1988):

> When I chainsawed my victims, Fred Olen Ray would stand right next to the camera, throwing body parts at me and splashing my face with Dixie cups full of blood, while a prop guy was squirting more blood all over my body. For my death scene, they used a mail order female chest filled with fake blood and guts, and then just chainsawed it right down the middle.

Hollywood Chainsaw Hookers was both Michelle's and producer Fred O. Ray's most notorious film. In it, a detective tracks a runaway girl (Linnea) to an ancient Egyptian cult of prostitutes, who gain immortality by sacrificing their clients with chainsaws. Ray notes, "The foreign mar-

Linnea Quigley, Gunnar Hansan and Michele Bauer pose for a publicity shot for *Hollywood Chainsaw Hookers*

ket was drying up because of censorship of sex and violence, and that kept us from selling a lot more rights overseas." Ironically, on UK movie posters, the word hookers was permissible yet chainsaw was forbidden, so it reads *Hollywood Hookers* with a small image of a chainsaw slapped on.

Fred Olen Ray, founder of American-Independent Productions, has been called the heir to grade-B filmmakers like Roger Corman and Samuel Z. Arkoff. According to Bruce G. Hallenbeck:

Fred Olen Ray promotes *Scream Queen Hot Tub Party*

Over the past two decades, Fred Olen Ray has ground out
more low-budget, schlock horror/sf/action pictures and
accumulated a more impressive list of directing and/or
producing credits—at least in terms of quantity and variety—than any other living American filmmaker, exploi-

Attack of the B Queens

tation or otherwise. So, if anyone has earned the title Roger Corman once held as the American exploitation cinema's "King of the Bs," it surely must be Fred.

As a teenager, Fred taught himself the craft by making homemade monster movies with his family's 8-mm camera. During a job at a Florida television station, he made 16-mm movies on the side. Arriving in Hollywood in the early 1980s, he began working full-time on 35-mm film production and distribution. His breakthrough movie was probably *The Tomb* (1985). It was economically made for $135,000 and it earned three and a half million, saving investor Trans World Entertainment from bankruptcy.

From 1988 to 1992, I greatly enjoyed working with Fred as one of his stock players in almost a dozen movies, including *Warlords* (1988), *Mob Boss* (1990), *Bad Girls from Mars* (1991) and *Spirits* (1992). He challenged and encouraged me to grow as a dramatic and comedic actress, and so he was largely responsible for my horror fame today.

Haunting Fear (1991) was a particularly intense experience. It required me to get buried in a cellar, claw my way out of a coffin, transform into a bloody homicidal maniac, and slay several well-deserving victims. Fred wrote the script himself in only three days, and the movie was shot in six at a cost of $115,000. He adds:

> It's story-driven without a lot of gimmicks, except for the casting of a name-actor, Jan-Michael Vincent. I hired him for one day; that gave the film a glossier veneer and deluded people into thinking that I'd spent some money on it.

Nightmare Sisters

David DeCoteau, another '80s independent filmmaker, also played a big hand in making cult stars of Linnea, Michelle and myself. He worked as a projectionist at a movie theater in Portland, Oregon, saving his money to move to Los Angeles. Pestering Roger Corman for a job, he got work as a production assistant for James Cameron, an art director at that time. For a while, he switched to a different area of cinematic exploitation, the adult film business; by age 24, David had directed almost 40 hard-core movies and got burned out.

In 1986, he teamed up with Charles Band to produce his first legit feature, *Dreamaniac*. Band also financed *Creepazoids* (1987), featuring Linnea in a sexy shower scene and later battling a giant mutant rat. After uniting our trio for *Sorority Babes* and *Nightmare Sisters*, DeCoteau continued to cast Linnea and Michelle in other films. He and I co-produced a 4-volume horror documentary, *Shock Cinema* (1991), to share the inner workings of our trade. Under his own name and the pseudonyms Ellen Cabot and Victoria Sloan, Dave DeCoteau has produced and/or directed dozens of low-budget, high-profit features, including *Dr. Alien* (1988), *Murder Weapon* (1988), *Puppet Master III* (1992) and *Beach Babes from Beyond* (1994). DeCoteau's association with Band still continues, largely in exotic foreign locations like Romania.

Charles Band established himself as a force to be reckoned with in 1984, when he founded Empire Entertainment, although he started making exploitation films as early as 1972. Churning out cheap but satisfying schlock, he released 15 or 20 new pictures a year in the 1980s. It was Band who originated the goofy-title craze of B movies, insisting, "A title is very, very important. You have to come up with key words like psycho, bimbo or slut." Like *Space Sluts in the Slammer, Assault of the Killer Bimbos* and my own film, *Slave Girls from Beyond Infinity* (1987).

Critic Lewis Beale notes, "His productions have now taken on their own distinctive look and feel, consisting of self-parodic humor, comic-strip vitality, narrative simplicity, and a colorfully imaginative style." Charles Band adds, "No one sets out to make a bad movie. But if you

make a bad horror movie, it's still fun, because you still enjoy watching the monster get the girl. As long as certain elements are intact, people will watch it. And people are so jaded that humor has been injected as a release valve." A few Empire pictures of note are *Ghoulies* (1984), *Trancers* (1984), *Troll* (1985), *Crawlspace* (1986), *Cellar Dweller* (1987) and *Dolls* (1987). *Puppet Master* (1989) was one of the first productions from Full Moon, the company Band set up to replace his financially troubled Empire.

Another prolific B movie producer is Jim Wynorski, who has been called "the Russ Meyer of horror-fantasy," due to his fondness for casting pneumatic women. His films have starred an honor roll of shapely actresses: Traci Lords, Becky Le Beau, Raven De La Croix, Monique Gabrielle, Gail Robyn Harris, Tanya Roberts, Antonia Dorian, Barbara Crampton, Kelli Maroney, Heather Locklear, Lana Clarkson and Nicole Eggert.

I first met Jim in 1981, after shooting Corman's *Slumber Party Massacre*. At the time, he was working for New World as an advertising director and editor of movie trailers. He still collaborates frequently with Corman, and has also teamed up with Fred O. Ray, most notably for *Scream Queen Hot Tub Party* (1993) and *Dinosaur Island* (1994).

His first feature as a director was *The Lost Empire* (1986). He followed it with another 40 or so stylish films, filled with snap and menace and lots of folks with their clothes off: *Chopping Mall* (1986), *Death Stalker II* (1987), *Not of this Earth* (1988) and a string of sequels like *The Return of Swamp Thing* (1988), *Body Chemistry 2* and *3* (1993/94), *Ghoulies 4* (1992) and the delightful *976-Evil II* (1990), which has an amazing scene where a character is sucked into a TV set and finds himself part of *It's a Wonderful Life*, which suddenly makes a clever and horrific flop to *Night of the Living Dead*.

One of my favorite Wynorski films is *Transylvania Twist* (1989), a hysterical horror-satire starring Teri Copely and Monique Gabrielle. Jim offered me a bit part as a vampire, where I neck in a graveyard and die by unwittingly drinking a flask of holy water. Ever since my misspent youth watching those glorious Hammer horror movies, I've been a big fan of the vampire genre.

In the early '80s, I was sad to see vampires get lost amidst all the slasher films. But just to show you can't keep a good bloodsucker down, vampires were soon revived yet again in a rash of mainly youth-oriented pictures. *The Hunger* (1983) was a big-studio offering with high production values.

On a smaller note, timely Empire released *I Married a Vampire* in 1984. It was followed by *Fright Night* (1985), which did for vampires what *The Howling* did for werewolves; it re-established the commercial viability of the genre.

Also, new improved make-up effects did a lot to revitalize the usual clichés for the 1980s. Soon came *Fright Night II* (1988), *Vamp* (1986), *Graveyard Shift I & II* (1987/88), *The Lost Boys* (1987), *Vampire Knights* (1987) and *Near Dark* (1987), which proved to be one of the key horror films of the decade. Directed and scripted by Kathryn Bigelow, it had a memorable scene where white-trash vampires take over a bar to terrorize, kill, and drain a host of bikers, waitresses and thugs. The late 1980s gave us yet more style-conscious efforts, like *To Die For* (1988), Fred Olen Ray's *Beverly Hills Vamp* (1989), Anthony Hickox' vampire-Western *Sundown* (1989), *Teen Vamp* (1989), *Vampire's Kiss* (1989), and a big-budget culmination in 1992's *Bram Stoker's Dracula*.

Werewolves have also been a popular topic, ever since the classic Universal Studios pictures of the 1930s. When science fiction films gained momentum in the '40s, the werewolf craze slacked off until the

***The Company of Wolves* was a beautiful and intelligent story.**

1980s. Director Joe Dante, an alumnus from the unofficial Roger Corman film school, gave the genre a tongue-in-cheek boost with *The Howling* (1980), so successful that it spawned six sequels by 1995. A year later, director/writer John Landis made *An American Werewolf in London* (1981), an intriguing film with terrific special effects. *Full Moon High* (1982) was a comedy spoof on 1950s movies like *I Was a Teenage Werewolf* as was *Teen Wolf* (1986) starring Michael J. Fox. From the UK came *The Company of Wolves* (1984), a beautiful and intelligent story. *Silver Bullet* (1985) and *The Monster Squad* (1987) wrapped up the werewolf subgenre for the decade.

Monsters in general have always been a mainstay of horror cinema, and the 1980s were surely no exception. A banner film came out in 1979, Ridley Scott's *Alien*, starring Sigourney Weaver. She embodied a new tough chick icon, rapidly becoming a strong female role model for others (like myself) to emulate. *Alien* took a simple B-movie plot and combined it with a moody atmosphere, suspense, alarming special effects, and high action. It caused a flood of '80s alien invader flicks, such as *Xtro* (1982), *Invaders from Mars* (1986), *Alien Predators* (1986), not to mention several sequels itself.

Other films seemed like throwbacks to the halcyon days of the 1950s, when lumbering monsters were always yearning for the pretty heroines. In Corman's *Humanoids from the Deep* (1980), the underwater creatures *did* get to commit rape, not to mention a lot of mayhem. Similarly themed *Blood Beach* and *Blood Tide* were also released that same year. Adrienne Barbeau shined in 1982's *Swamp Thing*, which ech-

oed a much earlier film, *Creature from the Black Lagoon*. After *The Bog* (1978), we also got *Terror in the Swamp* (1984), which featured a man in a pathetic giant rat suit. Toxic waste monsters also had a prominent run, starting with *Forbidden World* (1982), *Impulse* (1982), Troma's *The Toxic Avenger* (1985) and *C.H.U.D.* (1984), where hazardous radioactive waste turns derelicts who live in sewers into ravenous cannibals.

Horror filmmakers found the most imaginative uses for dolls, often transforming harmless toys into murderous little monsters. Perhaps it was Karen Black's chilling segment in 1975's *Trilogy of Terror* that created a subgenre of killer toy movies. Stuart Gordon's *Dolls* (1987) led the way to *Child's Play* (1988) and its many '90s sequels, all featuring an evil Chucky. Close on its heels came *Death Doll* (1988) and seven of Full Moon's *Puppet Master* films, where an alchemist makes deadly puppets who run amok.

Joe Dante's uproarious black comedy *Gremlins* (1984) gave us the wholesale trashing of a Capra-esque town by strange little creatures. It

Check out who makes a guest appearance in *Gremlins* with Hoyt Axton!

was a major boon to horror merchandising (figurines, dolls, T-shirts, bubble gum cards, etc.) and launched yet another trend of cute small beasties on the rampage: Empire's *Troll* (1985) and *Ghoulies* 1-3 series (1985-87), plus Corman's *Munchies* (1987) and its sequel *Munchie* (1992).

At a time when the genre had become dominated by maniacs and psychopaths, evil won out with cynical regularity. In fact, many important horror films of the 1980s actually *were* supernatural thrillers. *The Exorcist* bludgeoned our senses in 1973 and sparked a new demonology cycle. The late '70s focused on the forces of Satan trying to subvert world order in such films as *The Sentinel* (1976), *The Omen* (1976) and its two sequels (1978/81). The trend continued with *Incubus* (1981), *Mark of the Beast* (1981) and *The Entity* (1982), in which a sex-starved demon rapes a California housewife. Eighties movies gradually became even more intense, loaded with sometimes purely visual horror.

For comedy relief, *Ghostbusters* (1984) amused us and featured a gorgeous Sigourney Weaver, spectacular special effects and a brilliant script. Pure evil came back in another big-studio release *The Keep* (1984), while mega-low-budget *Witchboard* (1986) was a surprise success in theaters and paved the way for Linnea's *Night of the Demons* (1988) and

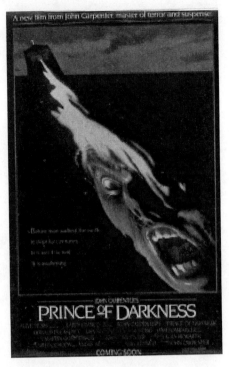

a 10-series run of *Witchcraft* movies (1988-97), plus three *Warlock* pictures (1988/93/99). One of my personal faves was John Carpenter's *Prince of Darkness* (1987); with its complicated plot and aura of menace, it was consistently eerie and fascinating.

Clive Barker's *Hellraiser* (1987) was unusually sober and tinged by human cruelty; its Grand Guignol intensity made it quite possibly the goriest R-rated film ever given a wide theatrical release. Jason Collum notes:

> The footage Barker cut to get the R-rating was re-inserted
> in one of the industry's first unrated videos. It was made
> available to viewers in both versions.

Its sequel *Hellbound: Hellraiser II* (1988) gave us still more wanderings in the gloomy passages of Hell.

The Amityville Horror (1979) reinvented the haunted house/ghost trend, leading to seven sequels. Spielberg produced Tobe Hooper's *Poltergeist* (1982), followed up by two sequels of more slimy creatures designed by horrormeister H.R. Giger. A series of four *House* movies (1986

"...The most tenaciously original horror film of the year..."

THE EVIL DEAD

to 1991) were refreshingly non-threatening, as was Tim Burton's extraordinary *Beetlejuice* (1988), a hilariously warped and intriguing work of art.

I'm often asked by fans to name my favorite horror film. I'd have to say it's Sam Raimi's entire *Evil Dead* (1982) series, all starring Bruce Campbell. *Evil Dead II* (1987) was less a sequel than an elaborate remake, leading to *Army of Darkness* in 1993. *Evil Dead* became an instant drive-in classic, although in Great Britain, copies were seized and destroyed. It probably influenced just about everything in the mid-'80s and contributed to a resurgence of the zombie subgenre.

The plot was basic, yet effective. Quoting from a great reference book, *The Encyclopedia of Horror*: "A group of five college students arrive for the weekend at a spooky tumble-down house in the wilds of Tennessee. There, they find an ancient book which has apparently been used to summon up a pack of demons. By the time dawn arrives, the sole survivor is Campbell." The staging was absolutely terrific, and Raimi won acclaim for his creative use of camera angles: virtuoso traveling shots and demon's eye views. I was well-entertained by its stylish direction and humorous undertones, and I consider it a rare gem.

The 1980s didn't last forever, of course (probably about 10 years) and the tremendous surge of direct-to-video products hit a major slump in the early 1990s due to a glut of B titles and the rise of ultra-conservative megachains like Blockbuster (or Lackluster, as I call it) Video. We saw the rise and fall of the independent studios, and now self-righteous political groups are targeting video as the latest scapegoat of society's evils.

Although the thrill is mostly gone, it was truly incredible while it lasted. I feel so awed and thankful to have played such a celebrated role in the whole 1980s horror phenomenon. It was *my* decade, and I will always cherish it.

Attack of the B Queens

SEQUELS A-GO-GO:
The Nightmare '90s
by Debbie Rochon

The 1980s were the supreme slaughter film era. Some of the most memorable horror flicks ever made were assaulting our movie houses and overheating our VCRs during that time. As a matter of fact VCRs themselves were just becoming a regular home appliance at that point. Staples of life in the '80s included a stove, a fridge, a shower, junk stocks, a TV and a VCR.

Then, along with the economy, the horror movie market crashed big time. By 1990 the psycho-stalkers (Jason, Freddy, Leatherface, Michael, Pinhead, et al.) were appearing less and less on the big screens and soon became nothing more than direct-to-video villains. Small studios that specialized in producing horror flicks (i.e., Cannon Films, Lightning Pictures, Empire, New World, to name only a few) would soon find themselves closing shop and either reinventing themselves as family film companies or producers of the soon to be popular erotic thrillers.

The beginning of the '90s saw the horror film fan hanging around his (it was still mostly men at that juncture) local video store twiddling his thumbs, praying for a new gore-infested release to ooze through the door. Sadly, he ultimately did more waiting than watching. Along with the new direction the video market was taking, it also saw a whole new type of B Queen. *Playboy* Bunnies, *Penthouse*

Pets and the like were finding a new and wonderful marketplace to work in; the sexy thriller made-for-cable movie. The traditional low budget horror movie actress would have to acclimatize herself to this new world order, or lay low and wait for the inclement casting calls to pass. Of course for the Bunnies and Pets this was open season for them to hop from sexy magazines to sexy movies. With cable channels becoming as popular and commonplace as the networks, and with the new and seemingly unlimited need for movies to fill late-night slots, the independents and B producers found a new golden goose.

The erotic thriller would eventually play itself out, but for at least the first half of the 90s the horror genre would have to settle for mostly rehashing the tried and true titles, meaning of course, banking on the *beast*...also know as The Sequel.

Although sequels have been moneymakers for decades prior to the '90s (I daresay the average viewer would be hard pressed to tally *exactly* how many *Nightmare on Elm Streets*, *Friday the 13ths* and *Halloweens* have been made) this was indeed an era of reanimating any celluloid fiend with a following. Some of these flicks even boast now-famous folks in their cast lists; *Critters 3* (1992) has mega-star Leonardo DiCaprio, *Critters 4* (1992) costars Angela Bassett—and even Johnny Depp, who appeared in the first *Nightmare* movie in 1984, resurfaced in the 1991 sequel *Freddy's Dead: The Final Nightmare*. (Remind me later to tell you about the so-called final thing.) Our gorgeous gals of gore films have occasionally reappeared themselves and fought back against even the most recurring, unstoppable ghouls. There was still a constant, albeit moderate, flow of fear flicks being made, but mostly with medium to big budgets—meaning $2-3 million or more.

I will take a moment now and give credence to the few horrors that surfaced during the lean years—*most* of which were not dependent on previously known titles. Anjelica Huston, in this author's opinion, was

born to play Morticia in *The Addams Family* (1991) and *Addams Family Values* (1993). She nailed the character's bland disposition toward life yet totally thrilled-to-death-about-the-afterworld persona. Christina Ricci was on the money herself as the deadly deadpan daughter. Who would have guessed such beauty was hiding under those pigtails? Kathleen Kinmont tore up the scenery (literally) in *Bride of Re-Animator* (1991), and Tracy Scoggins fought a malevolent baby doll and jack-in-the-box in *Demonic Toys* (1991). Lynn Redgrave *almost* saved the movie *Midnight* (1991) playing an Elvira-style TV horror hostess, but the script was neither campy enough nor scary enough for even a Redgrave to redeem. Jodie Foster broke new ground by winning an Oscar for her role in (a horror movie!) *Silence of the Lambs* (1991). Co-author Brinke Stevens co-starred in *Transylvania Twist* (1991), which was more of a spoof flick that serious scare-fare. *Army of Darkness* (1992) featured the fair maiden Bridget Fonda, but again this third installment in the *Evil Dead* series was far more for laughs than gasps. The mega-huge budgeted, but bloody-beautiful, *Bram Stoker's Dracula* (1992) was yet another Gothic vehicle for Winona Ryder. A more effective vampire flick for me was *The Addiction* (1995), starring Lili Taylor who was nominated in the Best Actress category for the Independent Spirit Awards in 1996. Mindy Clarke brought undeniable sex appeal to her zombie look in *Return of the Living Dead 3* (1993). In the third remake of *Not of the Earth* (1996) Elizabeth Barondes gave both her predecessors (Beverly Garland in 1957, Traci Lords in 1988) a run for their money as Nurse Amanda. Patty Mullen exposed her deft comedy skills in the offbeat and refreshing *Frankenhooker* (1990). Ultra-famous music gals Twiggy,

Deborah Harry and Sheena Easton indulged themselves in graveyard humor and bloody gore in the anthology *Body Bags* (1993). The lovely Kristy Swanson starred in a film that has inspired a TV series since; *Buffy the Vampire Slayer* (1992). A real underground gem, *Blood & Donuts* (1995) shows that sexy and talented actresses can come from Canada too, namely Helene Clarkson. To say Anna Falchi from *Cemetery Man* (1995) is pretty, is like saying Stephen King is a mildly successful novelist. If anyone had a shot at changing the lead actor Rupert Everett's mind about being gay (in real life), *she* would. *From Dusk 'till Dawn* (1995) featured a very Hollywood cast which included the pro-

lific Juliette Lewis, who first garnered attention in the 1991 remake of *Cape Fear*. Hammer Films siren Veronica Carlson headed the cast in the anthology *Freakshow* (1995) and proved to anyone who saw this feature that she still has it. Michelle Pfeiffer even got on the horror-hay-wagon and made *Wolf* (1994). One of today's top box office stars, Renee Zellweger, made *Texas Chainsaw Massacre 4: The Next Generation* (1995) which was released seconds before she skyrocketed to fame in the mainstream market. Another 1970s star, but in the Blaxploitation genre, Gloria Hendry popped back into the scene with *Pumpkinhead 2: Blood Wings* (1994). Which brings up an interesting question...why are so few African-American actresses in horror movies? The only actresses that come to my mind are Cynthia Bond in *Def by Temptation* (1990), Angela Bassett in *Vampire in Brooklyn* (1995) and Priscilla Basque in *Bugged!* (1996). There's definitely a few I've overlooked, but let's hope things change and we see many more talented and beautiful horror-lov-

This summer, terror won't be taking a vacation.

JAMIE LEE CURTIS

H 2 O

HALLOWEEN

TWENTY YEARS LATER

IN THEATRES EVERYWHERE AUGUST 5TH

ing African-American actresses gracing our screens. As far as I can determine none of our famous foes are racist, they hate and kill everyone equally. Ain't America grand?

In 1978 Jamie Lee Curtis worked with the man who would have the most lasting impact on her career, longer than any other; Michael Myers in *Halloween*. Heeding the success of recent horror films in Hollywood and with a comfortable paycheck, she teamed up with Myers again for the 1998 release *Halloween H20* and 2002's *Halloween: Resurrection*. Although *H20* never garnered the critical acclaim the first of the series did, it made millions of dollars at the box office nonetheless, and was proof positive that we haven't yet got enough of that masked guy, plus we care about what happened to our heroine from 20 years ago. Does that make us sadistic splatter film fans with heart? I think most horror movie fans check the "Yes I want to be an organ donor" box on the back of their driver's license. If I drove I would, but that's only if they were absolutely sure I didn't need the organ anymore before they removed it.

What differentiates the late 1990s horror movie box office sales and video rentals from any other decade is the spending power of women. The typical horror movie patrons from yesteryear were, of course, men, with the occasional arm-gripping gal-pal who would spend the bulk of the movie peeking from behind her hands. Not so today. With the totally liberated, in-control, financially and emotionally independent woman of the '90s comes a new and glorious fan base for the terror genre. Today's horror movie heroines must now appeal not only to the guys watching but the chicks too. While throughout horror's history a female character

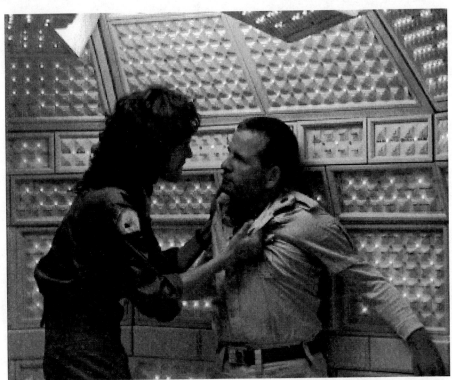
Sigourney Weaver as the assertive Ripley in *Alien*

would be one of the very few (if not the only one) who would live to the end credits, in today's market she must display charisma from the neck up as well. Don't get me wrong, she can still do her share of screaming and heavy breathing during her 90-ish minutes on celluloid, but she must also be convincing in her role, not just in her sweater. Reflecting this trend, women's roles have become much more assertive, for example Sigourney Weaver in the *Alien* series.

To make the ultimate list of horror movie actresses in the 1990s is a difficult if not impossible task. It really comes down to a matter of taste and opinion. One critic's favorite screamer can be like bloody nails on a chalkboard to the next critic. So if there's a glaring omission on my part I apologize in advance, but one can't list every actress who has appeared in a horror movie in the 1990s. Also, there are countless actresses who make a living in this genre on other continents, but I'll be dealing almost exclusively with American beauties. To qualify the list one would have to break it down into categories. The mainstream Scare Queens and the low-budget/independent-level B Queens.

The "It's Now Cool To Be In A Horror Movie" Scare Queens Category

A number of Hollywood/TV celebrities have worked in the fear franchise sometimes prior to their boob tube success and sometimes during. *Friends* star Jennifer Aniston led the unlucky cast in *Leprechaun* (1993), which spawned 3 sequels... so far. *The Party of Five* sitcom boasted today's most famous horror queen Neve Campbell. In 1996 she made *The Craft* and the (now) sequel crazy *Scream*, which also starred *Friends* babe Courtney Cox. Neve reprised her role in *Scream 2* (1997) and kept her vocal cords in ship-shape by appearing in *Scream 3* (1999). The director, Wes Craven, has become the king in Horror-wood being touted as the man who single-handedly resuscitated the horror movie as a serious money maker. The *Scream* series was not only genuinely terrifying, but had a wonderful sense of mimicking the knife-wielding stalker-movie genre in a very clever way.

In case anyone reading this actually thinks this was the first of its type (i.e., a scary slasher flick with scary slasher movie in-jokes), I must bring to attention Rolfe Kanefsky's 1991 flick *There's Nothing Out There*.

Kanefsky's attempt, like *Scream*, features a well-versed horror-aholic character who has memorized every slice-'em-up film released on video, and recognizes the signs that foreshadow doom. Of course the other characters dismiss his concerns as the workings of a person who watches too many videos, but there really is something out there, and the teens begin experiencing an attrition problem when they start stumbling into all the clichés found in a typical teen horror film.

Another *Party of Five*r who got big scream attention was Jennifer Love Hewitt, who starred in *I Know What You Did Last Summer* (1997) and (not to be outdone) *I Still Know What You Did Last Summer* (1998). Yet another TV teen idol named Jennifer (Aspen) from *Party of Five* dabbled in the macabre and added the sequel *Sometimes They Come Back...Again* (1996) to her resume. All the aforementioned TV stars have to be lumped together, with the exception of Aniston for obvious reasons, because these gals aren't the real deal. They're wonderful to watch run shrieking across the screen, but let's face the facts, they strictly did it for money and to be hip. It was like a virus, any-

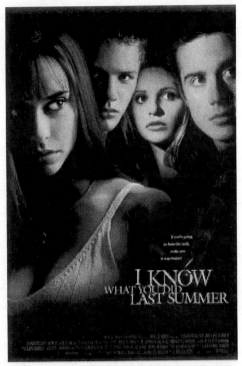

one that was anyone in a youth-driven top-five TV series was making a slasher movie, so every greedy agent worth his weight in gore got on the phone and after years of withdrawing in terror at the thought of one of their clients making a horror movie were now looking for scare-scripts! It's not to say that other B movie actresses wouldn't do it for the money, but let's get down to it...not one of these sitcom beauties had to get naked. Hey, don't get me wrong, some of the finest B movies ever made didn't show a single frame of nudity. I guess after watching horror movie starlets struggle for so many years I sympathize and relate to the actresses who performed nude while covered in blood and brains just to keep the gas turned on for another month. And, most importantly, because they actually love horror movies! But I digress. Ahem.

Multiplex queen Drew Barrymore learned long ago the value of scare. The little *Firestarter* (1984) started the '90s by appearing in *Waxwork II: Lost in Time* (1992), which, for her bloodline was definitely slumming it somewhat. Finally I have to mention Jennifer (another one!) Tilly, who did a masterful job as Chucky's true love in *Child's Play 4* aka *Bride of Chucky* (1998). These are just some of the higher-paid actresses who found a frightening level of success in the 1990s.

The Low-Budget/Independent Horror Movie
(Appearing-Sometimes-Nude-But-Not-Always)
B Queens Category

This category will include actresses who have worked in horror movies that you catch on cable TV and can rent at video stores, but you'll rarely—if ever—see them billed in a feature shown in a theater. Now these B actresses will vary in description from the-almost-became-stars-but-didn't-quite-make-it gals, to the I-was-a-playmate-but-now-I-do-genre-films babes, to the I'm-just-here-till-a-real-role-gets-handed-to-me actresses. Whatever the circumstances that landed them in the killer's grasp, that's not really unimportant. The fact is, they have made enough of an impact in the genre to be noticed. Once again, this is just my opinion and I'm sure there are many dedicated fans out there who will be shocked that I never mentioned their personal favorite. The truth is many of the actresses that are highlighted in popular genre magazines and web sites are either transitory and don't sign onto more than one horror film or that some of the most popular *femmes fatale* are less horror movie actresses and more erotic thriller stars like Shannon Tweed for example.

Heather Langenkamp put a new spin on her role by playing herself in the seventh (we should never say final) installment of the *Nightmare* series: *Wes Craven's New Nightmare* (1994). While the film was only a mild success, it had a very complex and intelligent storyline. Heather never broke away from her *Nightmare* fame, and although she is a very solid actress, chances are, she will be associated exclusively with this series for the rest of her career. Ami Dolenz, daughter of Mickey Dolenz who was the drummer in the '60s pop group The Monkees, has starred in a number of mainstream movies but took the occasional pit stop in horrorville. *Witchboard 2* (1993) had Ami contacting the dead through an old Ouija board and opening one of the seemingly countless doors to hell. Maybe it's a good thing that she hasn't hung around for too long because Ami opens yet another gateway to hell in *Pumpkinhead II: Blood Wings* (1994).

William Shatner's progeny Melanie Shatner starred in a double header; *Bloodstone: Subspecies II* (1993) and *Bloodlust: Subspecies III* (1994). Both father and daughter shot an episode of the cable series *Perversions of Science* (1997) together. That sounds odd...I wonder if that's illegal...?

LLOYD KAUFMAN AND MICHAEL HERZ PRESENT A TROMA TEAM RELEASE

"EROTIC AND FRIGHTENING"

TROMA

The
Virgin Heart

Witchcraft

IV

DIRECTED BY
JAMES MERENDINO

FEATURING
JULIE STRAIN

TROMA
DVD
THE BEST
MOVIES
& THE BEST

Penthouse Pet and co-author Julie Strain, who is as equally associated with erotic features as she is hard-core horror, has also faced one of Satan's many escape hatches. In the mammogram-able *Witchcraft 4: Virgin Heart* (1992) Strain strips her way to saving the day not to mention the film. The same year Strain actually becomes the creature from hell in

The Unnamable 2: The Statement of Randolph Carter (1992), which also stars Roger Corman favorite Maria Ford, who is known for her sexy late night pictures aka the erotic thrillers. In *Slumber Party Massacre 3* (1990) Ford runs around in lingerie trying not to get drilled by a serial killer. Believe me, having to watch this serial should be what's killing off everyone.

Up and comer Eileen Daly starred in *Witchcraft X: Mistress of the Craft* (1998), yes folks that means it was the tenth one, before shooting the very well-received *Razor Blade Smile* (1998) which is a stylish up-to-date version of a Hammer Studios vampire film from the 1970s.

Another cable queen, Monique Parent, strolled the terror zone in *Blood Thirsty* (1997) and *Alien Escape* (1995) but she's more commonly associated with erotic videos. Chandra West has also made more of a mark in her mainstream efforts, but has wandered into the Band brothers' clutches and made *Puppet Master 4* (1993) and *Puppet Master 5: The Final Chapter* (1994). By the way, it was not the final chapter, there indeed was a part 6 called *Curse of the Puppet Master* (1998). Those evil filmmakers! Piece of advice: never believe it when the title says it's the final chapter. It's almost certain that if it says it is, it's not. Okay?

English stage actress Lysette Anthony graced the screen in the comedy *Dracula: Dead and Loving It* (1995), then went on to do the soon-forgotten *Trilogy of Terror II* (1996). Karen Black, who starred in the original *Trilogy of Terror* (1975), has continued to work in her horrific element; one of her latest credits include *Children of the Corn 4: The Gathering* (1996). Another horror staple, Dee Wallace, has also been working on her follow-up film list. Our *Cujo* (1983) gal starred in the lukewarm *Alligator II: The Mutation* (1991). Just the thought of that aqua gem gives me shivers down my spine.

Star of *Temptress* (1995), Kim Delaney, made a very big contribution to *Dark Man II: The Return of Durant* (1994)—see the film and you'll know what I mean. Countless other cable queens have paid the bills with stints in many of the horror movie sequels I've already mentioned; Stephanie Beaton in *Witchcraft IX: Bitter Flesh* (1996), Ashley Rhey in *Witchcraft 7: Judgment Hour* (1995) and Denice Duff was in at least 3 *Subspecies* sequels. These may not be the most frightening features around but you have to admit, they're keeping a lot of LA-based actresses in the green! The list could go on and on, but these are some of the higher-profiled horror queens of the '90s. I used the angle of The Sequel just to prove the point that where there's a good horror movie,

NEL 1979 "ALIEN" VENIVA DA DENTRO. NEL 1986 "ALIEN" SE NE ERA ANDATO PER SEMPRE. NEL 1992 LE PEGGIORI PAURE DIVENTANO REALTÀ... "ALIEN È TORNATO.

ALIEN³

there's a sequel. Well, I guess it should read: where there's money to be made there's a sequel. Seeing I'm a horror fan myself, I really don't like to look at it that way... But alas, so "B" the business.

INTO THE
POST-MODERN ERA:
The Past, Present and Future
by Jason Paul Collum

As the Me decade came to a close, the Scream Queen was in her prime. Linnea Quigley, Brinke Stevens and Michelle Bauer ruled the nest. Though most of their features were delegated to the video rack instead of the theater, these three lovelies had indeed obtained top cult status. Their name atop a video box cover guaranteed some healthy degree of sales, while appearances at horror and science fiction film conventions drew hour-long lines for autographs.

Quigley was undeniably the most popular of the three, verified by the extent of her work. Within one year (1989/1990), the actress accumulated 11 film credits, earning coverage in magazines from the genre-related like *Fangoria*, to the big time press of *Variety, Premiere,* and *People*. She had also managed to cross over to the comedy genre, appearing in the *Vice Academy* and *Assault of the Party Nerds* series, *Treasure of the Moon Goddess*, plus earlier efforts like the Cheech and Chong films of the early 1980s.

Stevens was the smart/business-minded member. With a Masters degree in Marine Biology (coupled with a continuous 4.0 G.P.A. and an ability to speak seven foreign languages), the German/Mongolian Stevens had literally become an actress by accident. She parlayed modeling gigs and roles in both A- and B-level films (from *Body Double, This is Spinal Tap* and *Three Amigos!* to *The Slumber Party Massacre, Sorority Babes in the Slimeball Bowl-A-Rama* and *Slave Girls Beyond Infinity*) into a fan club empire. She was able to sustain herself on income from her fan club alone, which hawked her photos, films, movie memorabilia such as wardrobe and set pieces and exclusive artwork. Whereas Quigley and Bauer simply appeared at the conventions, Stevens worked them. She took time to meet each and every one of her fans, and often responded personally to every single letter. In doing so, fans felt they knew the actress on a personal level, which in turn made them want to buy her autographed products to prove to their friends they knew her.

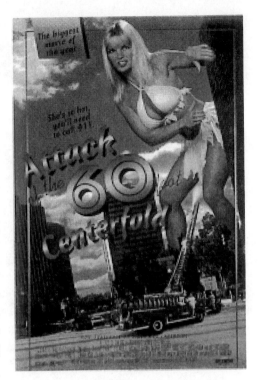

Bauer was the reluctant Scream Queen. In fact, it's a title she's often shot down and denied. A pin-up model in the late 1970s who went on to appear (under the moniker Pia Snow) in a number of erotic films like *Bad Girls* (1980) and the adult classic *Café Flesh* (1982), Bauer became a cult icon in the mid-1980s for her willingness to disrobe in low-budgeters like *The Tomb* (1985) and *Hollywood Chainsaw Hookers* (1987). Though Quigley and Stevens were obviously popular for the same reasons, Bauer was a favorite because of her tanned, smooth, statuesque form. She wasn't a cheerleader or a bookworm. She was the first girl at the high school party to slam down a beer bong and take on the guys in a game of strip poker. Bauer was always at her best when her role called for humor. Whether she was the obnoxiously overweight geek in *Nightmare Sisters* (1987), a cave-dwelling jungle girl in *Dinosaur Island* (1994), or the goofy head nurse in *Attack of the 60 Ft. Centerfold* (1995), it was always blatantly clear Bauer was a true comedian at heart.

If these girls were considered The Terrifying Trio, then vampy Elvira was their campy counterpart. Draped in a black, slit-to-there barely legal dress and beehive punk hairdo, the horror hostess (gleefully created and portrayed by Cassandra Peterson) originally cracked bad jokes about the often-terrible B movies she showed on her TV show *Movie Macabre*. The show was such a success she branched into a popular theatrical release, appropriately titled *Elvira, Mistress of the Dark* (1988), commercials, and over 100 guest spots on TV sitcoms and game shows. Her costume became the best-selling Halloween item in history, as did other

Julie Strain

holiday accessories like black lipstick, nail polish and even music CDs. Her live shows at amusement parks like Knott's Berry Farm frequently sold out, leaving crowds rolling with her off-beat sense of dry humor and Vegas-inspired dance numbers. Though relatively quiet on the movie and television scene during the late 1990s, she promised a major comeback with her second feature film, *Elvira's Haunted Hills* (2002), which put a humorous spin on the Edgar Allan Poe/ Roger Corman/Vincent Price films of the 1960s.

Waiting in the ranks during the end of the decade was a stunning model who was appearing on billboards and taking non-speaking roles in genre pics like *Repossessed* and *Naked Gun 33 1/3*. Standing 6 feet 2 inches, it was merely a matter of time before Julie Strain would catch the eye of producers more than willing to exploit her lean, busty frame. However, unlike most nubile youngsters who later complain they were taken advantage of by said producers, Strain was the one taking control. She wanted celluloid fame and knew her body was the way to attain it. In almost every feature she made throughout the 1990s and early 2000s, it was basically guaranteed she would not only strip down, but wind up in some sexual situation, often with both men and women. Her credits quickly rose to over 100 features, and, after marrying *Teenage Mutant Ninja Turtles* creator and *Heavy Metal* magazine owner Kevin Eastman, she would release an impressive volume of glamour books, photos and videos. Her image could be found on every imaginable product, from mouse pads, T-shirts and CDs to mugs, scores of internet sites and even her own brand of Wiggle-Vision trading cards. At the end of the decade and ready to consume the next, Strain was declared by Roger Corman to be "The Millennium Queen" and "The Queen of All Media."

Others who tried to follow suit to varying degrees of success were Debra Lamb (*Stripped to Kill II*), Monique Gabrielle (*Death Stalker II, Bachelor Party*), Samantha Phillips (*Phantasm II, Angel IV*), Gail "Robyn" Harris (*Sorority House Massacre II*), Debbie Dutch (*Dinosaur Island, Hard to Die*), Melissa Anne Moore (*Into the Sun*), Hope Marie Carlton (*A Nightmare on Elm Street 4: The Dream Master, The Stand, Slumber Party Massacre III*), Maria Ford (*Saturday Night Special* and

just about any Roger Corman effort of the past decade), Charlie Spradling (*Mirror, Mirror* and *The Doors*) and Antonia Dorian (*Ghoulies IV*). Then there was naturally top-heavy Becky LeBeau, who had appeared in a hefty number of B level horror and comedy flicks during the late '80s and early '90s. It wasn't until she began to tire of her film work when she came up with an idea to bring in some additional income. Little did she, or anyone else, expect the idea to turn into an empire.

LeBeau and her husband, Steve, developed a video series called *Soft Bodies*, in which LeBeau, and other bosomy ladies, shed their clothes and danced around to sexy music. Though not entirely original, as *Playboy* had been doing the same for nearly a decade, *Soft Bodies'* niche was the all-natural girls...no silicone allowed. The series caught on with mail-order viewers immediately, then Pay-Per-View, and made LeBeau into a soft-core/burlesque icon. Others tried to imitate her, but only LeBeau succeeded to such an extreme high.

With cheesecake a huge success, it seemed odd the mainstream wasn't giving it much attention. Realizing this was a market to be exploited, Frederick S. Clarke (whose *Cinefantastique* magazine was the original sci-fi periodical to deliver in-depth, controversial coverage of horror, fantasy and science fiction films) melded forces with journalist Bill George in 1992 to create *Femme Fatales*. The magazine, which focused largely on the women of the same mediums, was a cleaner version of *Playboy*. Sales rose rapidly, resulting in the magazine's publication from quarterly, to bi-monthly, monthly, then every three weeks. Others soon followed suit, like *Scream Queens Illustrated, Draculina, Focus* and, later, in 2002, *Sirens of the Cinema,* a practical knock-off of *FF,* which was really a joining of the previous mags.

Genre companies were also flying high. Full Moon, founded in 1989 out of the rubble of Empire Pictures, had struck a distribution deal with Paramount and was at the height of its success with the first three *Puppet Master* films, the original *Subspecies* trilogy, and the growth of its *Trancers* franchise, featuring the likes of Helen Hunt (*Twister*), Thelma Hopkins (*Family Matters*), Denise Duff (*The Young and the Restless*) and Megan Ward (*Wayne's World*). The direct-to-video hits spawned big-budget movies like *The Pit and the Pendulum* (1991), *Shrunken Heads* (1994) and *Dragonworld* (1994). Other independent producers were raking in the cash from over-done franchises and the need for more programming as new cable networks exploded. Then came the fallout.

The low-budget movie market came crashing down in 1994. Tired of unoriginal genre flicks and endless sequels, audiences decided horror was no longer cool. To make matters worse, video store shelves were more than full, to the point where Blockbuster and other video chains put out numerous bins of used tapes at $5 or less. Additionally, the big blue franchise, and others like it, had gobbled up all of their smaller counterparts. Grocery stores, gas stations and corner marts were quickly dissolving their video racks, turning the space into vegetable stands and cigarette racks. Erotic thrillers were the only genre-related features to thrive, taking hold of the marketplace thanks in most part to *Basic Instinct* (1992), *Fatal Attraction* (1987), *The Hand that Rocks the Cradle* (1991) and the indie hits *Poison Ivy* (1992) and *Inner Sanctum* (1991). Along with the fall of the video market went the Scream Queens.

Most scream queens either retired (J.J. North—*Attack of the 60 Ft. Centerfold, Hybrid*), turned to porno (Teri Weigel—*Cheerleader Campe*—and Kim McKamy, aka Ashlyn Gere—*Creepozoids*), or struggled in cheapo shot-on-video films. The title was further destroyed by hordes of scantily clad ladies appearing in vampire costumes at horror conventions. These gals labeled themselves scream queens, even though they had never appeared in a single film or even video. If the Polaroids on their tables weren't selling, they'd offer fans some special

Amy R. Swaim, Roxanne, Debbie Rochon and Jennifer Peluso appear in
Hellblock 13.

attention in a back staircase or bathroom stall for a few extra bucks. The acts degraded both the moniker and the conventions, and soon each was being considered a waste of time.

The few to survive the B movie fallout were Brinke Stevens, Maria Ford, Julie Strain (who had gained further national attention with her image on the box art for *Witchcraft IV: Virgin Heart*), Samantha Phillips and Shannon Tweed. Roger Corman's girls, including Ford, Lisa Boyle and Julie K. Smith also maintained steady work, but not to the degree of the previous decade.

Concorde-New Horizons (originally known as Concorde, and changed again in 2000 to New Concorde) went from an almost all-horror slate in early '90s (thanks to four-million-dollar hits like *Carnosaur*, an impressive number for a low-budget movie) to practically none in the mid to late '90s, concentrating only on erotic thrillers and family films. In fact, erotic thrillers spilled onto the scene to the point of nausea between 1993 and 1998. Themes typically included the mysterious woman who came into the secure family unit, killed the wife and disassociated the father from his female children. A good portion of the films offered Shannon

Tweed above the title, and their usual distributors were Concorde, Prism and Full Moon, which hid behind the...label.

Most long-lived direct-to-video sequel series (*The Howling, Prom Night, Sleepaway Camp, Slumber Party Massacre, Silent Night, Deadly Night, ad infinitum*) had perished, leaving room for only a couple like *Puppet Master, Leprechaun* and *Children of the Corn* to amble along at unenthusiastic paces. Even top batters Leatherface, Michael Myers, Jason Voorhees and Freddy Krueger were, for the most part, buried by decimated box office returns. In the wake of the horror backlash, the few genre pics to appear from 1994 to 1996 were largely ignored (like 1994's excellent and underappreciated *New Nightmare*) and hung out to die miserable box-office deaths.

Full Moon continued to be the only truly successful genre company. Since it was one of the few to even concentrate on the horror genre, it owned most of the market with few competitors. However, in later years, the company fell on extremely hard times, laying off almost every employee as a result of lower production values and a monopolization by Blockbuster. A so-called "profit-share program" had been introduced by Blockbuster and other franchises, forcing most studios to sell movies to them at an average of $4 per tape, giving them a cut of the profits at a much later date. While big studios like Paramount and Universal were able to appease the corporations which used the same method, smaller ones, who depended on immediate income, were hit hard. With mom and pop stores no longer in business, distribution companies had to give in to the pressure to go along with profit-sharing. The end result put many minor labels out of business.

A-Pix was Full Moon's only true competitor during the mid-to-late '90s. Releasing a number of d-t-v hits like *The Fear* (1994) and *Little*

Witches (1996) launched the company to the top of the indie charts. It picked up the *Witchcraft* franchise after indie label Academy Entertainment folded, and continued the trend of placing *Playboy* Playmates, like Alisa Christensen, in each installment. The series was promised an end with 1995's *Witchcraft VII: Judgement Hour* (offering two separate box covers—one continuing the theme, the other hiding its sequel status), but the gimmick was such a success there now exists a *Witchcraft XI: Sisters in Blood*, now distributed by the series' own production company, Vista Street Entertainment. After getting too big for its britches, trying to sell bigger-budget features to the theatrical market (including a failed attempt to make *The Texas Chainsaw Massacre 5*) A-Pix, as well, fell victim to the market's corporate stranglehold.

Ironically, genre magazines like *Cinefantastique*, *Femme Fatales* and *Fangoria* did not feel the same sting. According to Tony Timpone, *Fangoria*'s editor of over 16 years, "*Fangoria*'s sales have always been consistent. Our big concern during the 1990s, and even today, has been expanding the magazine into more markets that have been prejudiced against us because of our content."

While Full Moon and A-Pix were enjoying success restricted to video store rentals, horror was basically considered dead to the mainstream. The only success, horror-wise during this period could be found on television, thanks to the success of *X-Files*. Spin-offs (*Millenium*) and rip-offs (*Freaky Links*) followed, but only *X-Files* succeeded (even spawning an impressive 1998 feature film) until creator Chris Carter pulled the plug himself after nine seasons, ending the series in 2002. Just as horror fans were coming to terms with the loss of their beloved genre, two little films arrived in theaters in 1996 (thanks to a big push by the 1995 teen hit *Clueless*), and the big-budget, theatrical horror film was reborn for a new generation.

In May 1996, Columbia Pictures released *The Craft*, a tale of four teenage girls, who dabble in witchery and discover they indeed have powers. With a cast of then-mostly unknowns (including Robin Tunney,

Fairuza Balk, Neve Campbell, Rachel True, Christine Taylor, Skeet Ulrich and Breckin Meyer), the film played directly to the ignored *female* teen-age demographic. The lead girls were outcasts, each with a negative impression of her own self worth. In finding their supernatural powers, they found their inner strengths and took control. In fact, *The Craft* was largely the beginning of the Grrrrl-power era, exemplified in the ensuing years by pop groups like the Spice Girls and Britney Spears, glittery T-shirts and MTV cartoons like *Daria*. Depressing grunge and Nirvana was out...pretty girls with attitude were (thankfully) in.

Hollywood had long believed the main audience for horror films was boys. They were wrong. *The Craft* accumulated an impressive box office to the tune of over $26 million. Oddly, major studios still weren't catching on, but the little guys were. Later that same year, just before Christmas, a national phenomenon occurred.

Dimension, an extension of art house pictures distributor Miramax, had languished since the early 1990s on trying, unsuccessfully, to milk money from familiar titles like 1992's *Hellraiser III* and *Children of the Corn II*. Then magic melded a witty self-referential slasher script by newcomer Kevin Williamson and famed horror director Wes Craven (*A Nightmare on Elm Street*), with two of *The Craft*'s leads (Campbell and Ulrich) to create *Scream*. Written in just three days, the story followed modern-day teens who knew how stupid slasher films of the 1980s often were, yet seemed to fall victim to the same predicaments. The major differences were 1). dark humor which poked fun at the film itself, and 2). these kids all talked and acted like adults. They were smart, well-dressed and hip. Additionally, the killer wasn't perfect. He wasn't a Jason Voorhees or Michael Myers who always knew where the next victim was hiding, and always managed to stay 30 steps ahead of his/her prey. The victimizer in *Scream* often fell, had to seek out the kids and waited for the heroine to lose her virginity before he attacked. Ultimately, sex, drinking and drugs, always the biggest no-no's in horror films of the previous decade, didn't result in death.

Scream did something else unique. It became more of a success as each week passed. For nearly two months, weekend totals found the feature topping the previous weekend's gross, eventually culminating in well over $107 million domestically. The lead cast, which also included Drew Barrymore, Courtney Cox-Arquette, David Arquette, Rose McGowan, Jamie Kennedy, Matthew Lillard and nifty cameos by Linda

DON'T ANSWER THE PHONE. DON'T OPEN THE DOOR. DON'T TRY TO ESCAPE.

THE HIGHLY ACCLAIMED NEW THRILLER FROM WES CRAVEN

SCREAM

DAVID ARQUETTE · NEVE CAMPBELL · COURTENEY COX · MATTHEW LILLARD · ROSE McGOWAN · SKEET ULRICH & DREW BARRYMORE

Blair (*The Exorcist*) and Henry Winkler (TV's *Happy Days*), instantly rose to the top of Hollywood's A-list. The horror film, and especially the slasher film, had been reborn.

Perhaps it was simply the need for the genre to go away for a while to allow it to come back as something fresh. *The Craft* and *Scream* rejuvenated the genre. *Little Witches, I've Been Waiting for You* and other "school girls dabbling in the dark side" films came back to ride their coattails. Television's *Charmed* debuted on the newly formed station The WB and brought to the small screen a near replica of the big screen's teen witches (here with Holly Marie Combs, Shannen Doherty and Alyssa Milano), going so far as to use the same theme music ("How Soon is Now?" by Love Spit Love). Advancing the trend were equally impressive box office takes with *I Know What You Did Last Summer* ($75 million), *Bride of Chucky* ($45 million), *Halloween H20: Twenty Years Later* ($55 million), and *Urban Legend* ($40 million). Of course the sequels *Scream 2* ($103 million), *Scream 3* ($80 million) and *I Still Know What You Did Last Summer* ($35 million) didn't exactly hurt matters.

In addition to a glut of theatrical slasher films from top studios, A-list scream queens arose. Anyone related to The WB or Fox, mainly Neve Campbell, Sarah Michelle Gellar, Jennifer Love Hewitt and Katie Holmes, were the Jamie Lee Curtises of the new generation. Curtis herself regained her throne with 1998's *Halloween H20: Twenty Years Later*, which had a box office staggering so high over the series' previous five chapters (only the 1978 original had a higher gross), it caught the entire industry off-guard. Others competing for the A-list throne were Rose McGowan (*Phantoms, Devil in the Flesh*), Reese Witherspoon (*Fear*), Brandy (*I Still Know What You Did Last Summer*), Ali Larter (*Final Destination, House on Haunted Hill*), Famke Janssen (*The Faculty, Deep Rising, House on Haunted Hill*), Alix Kromski (*Mimic, Mimic 2, The Haunting, Children of the Corn 666*), Clea DuVall (*Little Witches, The Faculty, Ghosts of Mars*), Jennifer Tilly (*Bride of Chucky*), Rebecca Gayheart (*Scream 2, Urban Legend, Urban Legends: Final Cut, From Dusk 'till Dawn 3*), Bridgette Wilson (*I Know What You Did Last Summer, House on Haunted Hill*), Salma Hayek (*The Faculty, From Dusk 'till Dawn*) and Katherine Heigel (*Bride of Chucky, Valentine*). A few guys such as Alexis Arquette, Matthew Lillard, Freddie Prinze, Jr. and Ryan Phillipe also vied for the title of Scream King.

Surprisingly, it was another two years before the B movie industry picked up on the fact that horror was indeed alive and well. It wasn't until nearly 2000 when direct-to-video slashers, from the decent *Lover's Lane, Final Stab, Do You Wanna Know a Secret?* to the horridly awful *Bloody Murder*, showed up on store shelves. Though direct-to-video horrors remained scarce from *Scream*'s heyday to *Halloween H20* and *Bride of Chucky*'s triumphant grips on the box office, it was a little $16,000 shot-on-video movie in 1999 which kicked the industry right in the gonads.

The Blair Witch Project officially kicked off the new swing in independent horrors. In addition to reinvigorating the 20-year-dormant subgenre of possession/witchcraft flicks (*Stigmata, Lost Souls, Soul Survivors*), *The Blair Witch Project* proved to Hollywood money could be made without expensive CGI and a controlling hand. Fresh ideas were, indeed, still untapped. Additionally, shot-on-video movies had typically been laughed at, often even said to not be "real movies." One hundred twenty-six million dollars domestic gross later, *The Blair Witch Project* had Hollywood biting its own serpent tongue.

MISSING

On October 21, 1994, Heather Donahue, Joshua Leonard and Michael Williams hiked into Maryland's Black Hills Forest to shoot a documentary film on a local legend, "The Blair Witch." They were never heard from again.

One year later, their footage was found, documenting the students' five-day journey through the Black Hills Forest, and capturing the terrifying events that led up to their disappearance.

THE BLAIR WITCH PROJECT

Soon after, and we're talking merely weeks, *The Blair Witch Project* spoofs and rip-offs flooded video shelves and internet sites. Within two months, over 80 had been counted. Spoofs from *The Blair Bitch Project* with Linda Blair and *The Blair Warner Project* (referring to Lisa Welchel's

character on TV's *The Facts of Life*), to erotica like *The Bare Wench Project 1—3* and *The Erotic Witch Project* to full-on pornography *The Queer Witch Project* and *The Bare Tits Project,* ran the gamut in creative taste and sleaze. Suddenly, everyone wanted to make a movie for no budget, but rake in the dough. Therefore, the B and C level Scream Queens were reborn/created.

Brinke Stevens, who had spent the last years of the '90s in a run of family features, returned to the top of the horror heap with a staggering 11 films in 2000, 10 in 2001 and over five projects already lined up in early 2002. Among those two dozen films: *American Nightmare, Witchouse 3: Demon Fire, The Frightening, Hell Asylum, Horrorvision* and *Real Time: Seige at the Lucas Street Market.* Stevens believes:

> In my early years, I built up a good reputation with both fans and filmmakers. As such, my name has remained in demand for over two decades. Also, many of my 13-year-old fans have since grown up to become writers and directors themselves, who now want to hire and work with me. It's a fun twist of fate where everybody wins!

Linnea Quigley also began to make a return from obscurity. After appearing in occasionally raunchy Jess Franco flicks with Michelle Bauer in late '90s, Quigley moved onto more artsy and respected fare with *Nerve, Kolobos* and others in the 2000s. She had moved to Florida in the mid-'90s to escape the suffocating L.A. culture and to be closer to her parents, but moved back to L.A. in 2002, presumably to hit the same market/trend Stevens had tapped into.

Michelle Bauer seems to be the only holdout. She had retired in 1997 with only occasional cameos in small comedies, mostly directed by Fred Olen Ray. Though not at all rude toward followers, Bauer remains out of sight. Also, while more than willing to be interviewed regarding her peers' careers, like David DeCoteau, Bauer politely refuses any questions in regards to her own career and current status, in most part to raise a family.

With Bauer and Quigley subdued, Debbie Rochon seemed to be Stevens' most recognizable competition for the throne. An actress who struggled both on the streets of New York City as a teenager and in no-budget flicks, like the unbearable *Santa Claws*, throughout most of her early career, Rochon finally hit her stride with a string of independent,

and better-publicized, 2000s horror films. She began to receive notice in a lineup of Troma films such as *Terror Firmer, Tromeo & Juliet* and *Citizen Toxie: The Toxic Avenger IV*, and the cult success *Abducted II*. Her most noted role, however, was in the 2001 slasher *American Nightmare*, in which she portrayed a mentally unstable woman who listens over the radio, to the fears of a group of friends on Halloween night. Later, she uses those same fears to torture and eliminate the kids.

Rochon found additional success in a series of films produced by J.R. Bookwalter (*The Dead Next Door*). With lead roles in the Full Moon-distributed movies, like *Witchouse 3, Killjoy 2* and *Dead and Rotting*, Rochon's exposure grew rapidly, making her face and name a better-known commodity and landing her additional jobs in indie efforts like *The Bog People* and *Dr. Horror's Erotic House of Idiots*.

Bookwalter, a young horror enthusiast who began making 8mm movies in the late 1970s while in junior high, has long been considered the King of Guerrilla filmmakers. (Definition: a person who shoots most of his movies on various video formats, and receives a minuscule distribution deal, if one at all, allowing for only the hardest of hard-core horror and movie fanatics to know they, and their movies, exist.) He had found cult success with his 1985, Sam Raimi–produced 8mm gore epic *The Dead Next Door*, which found a slightly wider release in 1989. In the early 1990s, he struck a deal with DeCoteau, who produced a slew of shot-on-video features with Bookwalter and his cohorts as the writers/directors. After their deal ended (with little profit), Bookwalter used his new understanding of the business and developed projects to shoot on a higher grade of video. Some of those features, like 1994's *Ozone* and 1996's *The Sandman*, found favor with critics. These, and his continued friendship with DeCoteau, landed Bookwalter a position at Full Moon. A few years later, he was finally directing movies shot on actual film.

There are worse projects an actress could do besides a Bookwalter film. His work had almost built up a subgenre of its own, and had the actresses to represent it. Frequent players included Ariauna Albright, Jennifer Huss and Barbara Katz-Norrod. As he garnered more clout, he was able to obtain the higher-end B actresses (Stevens and Rochon) plus other cult celebrities (Tina Krause). As he moved further into the 2000s, he had even worked with names like Brenda Bakke (*Tales from the Crypt: Demon Knight*), Andrew Prine (*The Town That Dreaded Sundown*) and William Shatner (*Star Trek*).

From the Bookwalter camp grew other production talents like Tammi Sutton (*Killjoy 2*) and Danny Draven (*Hell Asylum*). Draven brought something back to the indie horror scene, which had been missing for years—unabashed gore and hot chicks. Draven's films usually exemplified his high energy and MTV-inspired visuals to such an extreme extent, it frequently hid the fact that his films (which also brought a nasty edge back to the genre splatterhounds that had been missing) typically had no budgets.

Of course Bookwalter and Draven were not alone in their fields. Other underground filmmakers like Kevin Lindenmuth (*Vampires and Other Stereotypes*) and Tim Ritter (*Truth or Dare*), drew attention to their own collection of talents such as Sasha Graham (*Addicted to Murder*), Patricia Paul (*Wicked Games*) as well as Kathy Willets (*Creep*), the Florida housewife, who was being prostituted by her husband and later became a porno star.

Another market had also developed to appease an underground group of viewers. Long dormant because of the Political Correctness movement and political bullying, films laced with misogyny had all but vanished. No longer would films like *The Toolbox Murders* (1978), *I Spit on*

Tina Krause

Your Grave (1979), *Mother's Day* (1980), *Don't Go in the House* (1980) and *Don't Answer the Phone* (1981) see the light of day...or so politicians thought. Two kids from New Jersey changed the system, and created a new levels of tortured and violated scream queens. Tina Krause, Misty Mundae, Pamela Sutch, Liz Bathory, Lily Tiger, Debbie D. and Marie Mazur were just a few of the lasses being humiliated in the S&M series of videos put out by W.A.V.E. pictures, begun by William Hellfire and Joey Smack. Also known as Factory2000, titles included *The Electric Cord Strangler, Strangled Housewife 1-8* and *Chloroformed*. Each film typically found the ladies abducted, beaten, tied, strangled, tickled and asphyxiated repeatedly. After the Columbine Massacre in 1999, Smack and Hellfire set out to do something different...make a real movie.

Using most of the same actresses, excluding Krause (who had managed to work her way into B level features) and Debbie D., the boys delivered the black-comedy *Duck! The Carbine High Massacre* (1999), which blatantly said out loud what the majority of Americans were whispering in their living rooms regarding the tragic events. The controversial movie failed to catch on with the general public, but proved to other indie filmmakers Misty Mundae actually had talent...turning her into the top C-level sex queen of the 2000s.

Mundae left her onscreen beatings and stranglings behind, and began headlining features like *Playmates of the Apes* and *Misty Mundae:*

Mummy Raider for Seduction Cinema and E.I. Independent. The company, launched by Mike Raso as a distribution outlet for ignored/forgotten soft-core and horror flicks of the 1960s and '70s, found great success by filling the less-threatening void of campy horror and action T&A pics based on hit movies. Mundae ruled the nest, with sassy unknowns like Darian Caine as her frequent sidekicks. Debbie Rochon occasionally tackled the more dramatic roles, while other soft-core divas such as Shauna O'Brien made appearances for bonus boobage.

On the other side of genre, David DeCoteau noticed the rest of B industry still wasn't really picking up on the teen horror trend Hollywood had begun exploiting. He left the coziness of Full Moon, where he'd been steadily employed since the late 1980s, and formed his own production company Rapid Heart Pictures in 1999. Taking aim directly at the teen market, he produced a series of horror films including *Ancient Evil: Scream of the Mummy* (2000), *The Brotherhood* (2000), *Final Stab* (2001), *The Brotherhood II: Young Warlocks* (2001), *The Frightening* (2002) and *The Brotherhood III* (2002). By striking a deal with Regent Entertainment giving his films much higher budgets than the average B movie, DeCoteau was able to sell most of his films as exclusives to Blockbuster, making his films possibly the most attainable in the current B video market. The plots of his films weren't overly unique, but DeCoteau, who had built his own reputation as a master of T&A in the 1980s and '90s, was determined to make his films stand out in another way.

While the average B film typically finds some way to get its female cast undressed and wet, David DeCoteau found ways to undress the male cast members. His strategy was to aim for the underexploited female demographic and gay male audiences. Though never actually naked, the boys in DeCoteau's films always walked around in underwear, took showers and exercised. They were Adonises, with perfect bodies and faces. Still, DeCoteau knew it would be unwise to completely exclude eye candy for the straight male viewers, so he began hiring some of the prettiest

Jacqueline Lovell

young girls in Hollywood, who had yet to receive notice (and likewise hoped they would, so he could exploit their names at a later date). Debra Mayer, Stacey Scowley, Elizabeth Bruderman, Melissa Renee Martin, Jennifer Capo and Tanya Dempsey were the chosen few, typically based on their flawless skin, sculptured bodies and innocent faces. Oh, and they could act, too.

Meanwhile, Universal had picked up a series of soft-core films directed throughout the late 1990s. Disguising itself behind the *Eros Collection* label, the company released features ranging from romantic comedies to erotic thrillers, many of which had aired on Cinemax (better known jokingly by the public as Sinemax and Skinamax). A set number of uninhibited young beauties made up the casts including Monique Parent, Maria Ford, Kira Reed, Kim Dawson, Shauna O'Brien, Vanesa Talor and Jacqueline Lovell, many of whom also frequented Full Moon's erotic videos. On a side note, Lovell, a perky blonde who could easily have played Cameron Diaz's little sister, turned her back on the industry, became a Born Again Christian, and reportedly invited all of her Hollywood chums to a backyard bonfire, made up of every video, magazine, book and poster she appeared in. She then returned to her home state of Florida and cut off contact with her former peers.

Though B-list Hollywood has slowly regained its footing within the first few years of the new millennium, A-list female *horror* stars are again gone. No more Jennifer Love Hewitts or Neve Campbells. By the early 2000s, theatrical audiences had been so saturated with dumb teen horror pics like *Valentine* and *Soul Survivors*, the genre's popularity rapidly began to plummet. In its place, though, grew more respected adult horror efforts like *What Lies Beneath* (2000), *The Others* (2001) and *Panic Room* (2002), which found A-list stars like Michelle Pfeiffer, Nicole Kidman and Jodie Foster happily appearing in movies more often referred to as thrillers. Though Jamie Lee Curtis did make her fourth appearance as heroine Laurie Strode in *Halloween VIII: Resurrection* (2002) (reportedly the result of her contract for *Halloween H20*), Hollywood's best-known ladies are steering clear of the horror label, though Johnny Depp seems determined to become the new Vincent Price. His only main competitor? Jeffrey Combs, a B-level cult celebrity for his 1985 classic film *Re-Animator*, who officially broke into the mainstream with A-list horror efforts like *House on Haunted Hill* and *I Still Know What You Did Last Summer*.

Meanwhile, women of color continue to remain scarce within any genre, especially at the B level. Seventies horror queen Pam Grier regained popularity in late 1990s thanks to high-profile roles in *Jackie Brown, Mars Attacks!* and *Escape From L.A.* Unlike many of her counterparts, Grier is a true cult icon, her name forever associated with the Blaxpoitation films of the 1970s and finally given respect in A-list films as her reward. Black cinema is slowly on the rise as well, with the success of New Line Cinema's *Friday* and *Next Friday*, though only Full Moon seems to have become aware of the plausible market at the B level. After their theories were proven correct by the unexpected success of the all-black *Killjoy* in 2000, the company assigned J.R. Bookwalter's camp duties to put out a hefty number of urban pics within the next year. Films like *The Vault*, *Ragdoll* and *The Horrible Doctor Bones* added additional success, with the Tammi Sutton-directed *Killjoy 2* moving some of the best numbers the company has seen in years. As a result of his popular *Hell Asylum*, which only had one black cast member, Danny Draven was signed to a four-picture deal, all of them urban-related. Though

Pam Grier has cohorts in a few other popular ethnic actresses like Halle Berry, Whoopi Goldberg and Vivica A. Fox, the B list appears to have a new queen...Olimpia Fernandez, who made her screen debut in *Killjoy 2* and already has four additional credits on her resume.

The A-list sexpot nest changes rapidly and is now ruled over by Shannon Elizabeth (*American Pie*), Angelina Jolie (*Tomb Raider*), Charlize Theron (*The Astronaut's Wife*), Jennifer Lopez (*The Cell*), Jaime Pressley (*Ringmaster*), Rachel Leigh Cook (*She's All That*), Jodi Lynn O'Keefe (*Halloween H20*), Kirsten Dunst (*Spider-Man*), Catherine Zeta-Jones (*Traffic*), Cameron Diaz (*Charlie's Angels*), Christina Applegate (*The Sweetest Thing*) and Tara Reid (*Urban Legend*). However, as the saying goes, "Here today, gone tomorrow." It should also be noted many of today sweethearts typically got their start in B-level films, typically horror. Who'll be the next girl to break through the barrier?

B Divas are definitely on their way back. Tanya Dempsey, Stacey Scowley, Debra Mayer, Melissa Renee Martin, Olimpia Fernandez, Daneen Boone, Holly Sampson, Tina Krause and Misty Mundae are among the up and comers in the video market. Mainstays from the 1990s

like Kira Reed (who has sex with her husband on a live website), Kim Dawson (who produced her own movie about being a soft-core actress against her best intents), Samantha Phillips (who busted out of soft-core into daytime TV with the one-season run of *Men are From Mars, Women Are From Venus*) and other favorites like Monique Parent, Shauna O'Brien, Julie K. Smith, Jillian McWhirter, Griffin Drew, C.C. Costigan, Amber Newman, Lorissa McComas, Shae Marks, Nikki Fritz, Tane McClure, Brinke Stevens, Linnea Quigley and Julie Strain continue their reign as the women who hold no shame is shedding their clothes before the camera, and bringing the fantasies of millions of men to celluloid realties.

As we head full force into the post-modern era, cinema has changed, and continues to evolve faster than ever. However, audiences are not as gullible. They want reality (as evidenced by the glut of camcorder TV shows). Self-referencing, so popular and consuming in American cinema only five years ago, is now passé. We are a trendier culture than ever before, and fads typically won't last more than 16 months. The DVD format is being forced on Americans who don't have the money to completely replace their already extensive videotape collections, yet are finding fewer options at Best Buy, Suncoast and other formerly VHS-friendly retail outlets. The good news, however, is that everything old is, indeed, new again. Forgotten cinematic drivel and B Queens of yesteryear can be found in the newest re-releases on DVD, often with cast interviews and making-of documentaries. Go out and rediscover the exciting worlds of the B movies, and the ladies who made them popular.

QUEEN BITCHES
OF THE UNIVERSE
by Melissa Miller

"Life's a bitch, now so am I."—Catwoman, *Batman Returns*

BITCH: A spiteful or lewd woman.
A complaint. *A difficult or confounding problem.*
—*The American Heritage Dictionary*

Over the years, the word "bitch" has developed into a misnomer. Women earning their own way in the world, making snap decisions and unfortunately acquiring the male ruthlessness gene are routinely referred to as bitches. Perhaps that is the correct word—for these women are definitely *a diffi-cult or confounding problem* to those around them.

This chapter will take a look at some of my favorite bitches, women who are un-mistakably an enigma to those near and not-so-dear, and their trials and tribula-tions from the 1920s to the present day. At times, the road's been rough but our versatile females transgressed it admirably. One can't help but admit that those feisty bitches are delightfully more fun than the typical hand-wringing namby-pamby heroines so prevalent in the movies.

"The Fearless Pearless Pearl White." In 1914 *The Perils of Pauline* turned Pearl White, an actress who starred in dramas and comedies for

Pathé, into the queen of the silent serials. Pearl did most of her own stuntwork, gamely allowing her director to impose untold tortures upon her, all the while managing to outwit a myriad of nefarious villains trying to do away with our plucky heroine, Pauline.

Pauline was the ward of a kindly guardian whose deepest desire was for his son Harry and Pauline to wed. But Pauline is no ordinary girl; she wants to see the world and have great adventures before settling down. Pauline's guardian dies and his evil secretary, Koerner, has gained control over Pauline's fortune. The dastardly Koerner spends the remaining 20 chapters using guns, trains, avalanches, fire, arrows, knives and any other form of malicious mayhem that crosses his evil little mind trying unsuccessfully to murder the adventurous Pauline.

Women were beginning to realize there was life beyond the kitchen... *The Perils of Pauline* helped point the way.

CATCH THIS WOMAN!
—Tricky Eyes, Dangerous Smile, Exquisitely gowned,
nimble fingers—she's *Outside the Law,* 1921

The life of the party and HOW!
—Clara Bow in *The Wild Party,* 1929

The Seven Deadly Whims
new lips to kiss
Freedom from conventions
A new world for women
No more chaperones
Life with a kick in it
The single moral standard
Our own latchkeys
—Gloria Swanson in *Prodigal Daughters,* 1923

The real Maria (Brigitte Helm) tries to save the children in *Metropolis*.

The 1920s—a swingin' time was had by all—especially at the movies. Douglas Fairbanks, Rudolph Valentino and Ramon Novarro set women's hearts aflutter. Tom Mix, Buck Jones and Hoot Gibson provided authentic cowboy action, Lon Chaney gave patrons the shivers, *especially* when an unsuspecting Mary Philbin removed his mask in *The Phantom of the Opera*, old dark house mysteries such as *The Cat and the Canary* and *The Bat* were the rage, Our Gang, Buster Keaton, Charlie Chaplin and Charley Chase made people laugh and Clara Bow, the "It" girl, was appearing in racily titled films such as *Dangerous Curves, The Wild Party, Rough House Rosie* and *The Fleet's In.* Gloria Swanson, Billie Burke and Mary Pickford routinely saw their name over film titles.

The robot Maria is burned at the stake for her sins in *Metropolis*.

Pickford, Chaplin and Fairbanks would eventually form United Artists, and America's sweetheart, Mary Pickford would retire a *very* wealthy woman.

In 1926 Fritz Lang would complete what is without a doubt his masterwork, *Metropolis*, a film that featured a saintly heroine and her robotic alter-ego, a depraved maniac who tries to lead the inhabitants of Metropolis to their doom. Lang and cinematographer Karl Freund created a terrifying glimpse of a future inhabited by haves and have-nots. The visionary set design and brilliant cinematography created an underground city populated by downtrodden workers and an above-ground paradise inhabited by a decadence-loving upper class. The lives of both

the workers and elite are controlled by the machinery needed to run the complex futuristic city. Perhaps screenwriter Thea von Harbou (a real-life bitch in every sense of the word) consulted her crystal ball before completing the script for *Metropolis*—unfortunately today, the have-nots still far outnumber the haves—with the gap widening every day.

While the script is often cited as quite silly, we do get to watch Brigitte Helm brilliantly run a gamut of emotions in dual roles (not from "A to B" as the witty Dorothy Parker noted of a Katharine Hepburn stage performance)—from saint to sinner as Maria, leader of the underground workers, who pleads with them to await a mediator to help them communicate with the above-ground elite, and as the pleasure-loving robotic double created by evil scientist Rotwang (Rudolf Klein-Rogge). Helm has a field day rolling her eyes, frenetically dancing with the upper-class, cavorting, carousing, causing riots and laughing hysterically as the hapless workers, realizing they have destroyed their children and homes (never for a moment considering they themselves made the error, placing the full responsibility on the impostor Maria [are we sure this film was made in 1926?]), burn her at the stake. She cackles with maniacal glee as the flames swirl around her and she meets a blazing end. Meanwhile, the real Maria and Freder (Gustav Froehlich) manage to save the children, evade Rotwang and bring about a peace between the laborers and the above-grounders. The astounding DVD restored *Metropolis* is breathtaking and only enhances the outstanding performance of Helm. With the Nazi influence growing in Germany, Lang would depart for the United States. Von Harbou would remain behind and become a good little Nazi.

SHE WAS NOT ALIVE...NOR DEAD
...Just a White Zombie—1932

WARNING! The Monster demands a Mate!
—*Bride of Frankenstein*, 1935

Look Out! She'll Get You!—*Dracula's Daughter*, 1936

The virtuous Maria would reflect the fast-approaching '30s. The party clothes were put away and the dress-down clothes brought out. The Depression was raging. A trip to the movie theater was a rare treat and not to be undertaken lightly. A visit to the local movie palace would probably be followed by a visit to the ice cream parlor for a 15-cent walnut sundae or a 5-cent lemon root beer. Film advertisements would be scrupulously inspected before the monumental selection of a film was made. Studios would indulge the public's desire to escape the despondent times—their taste for frivolity would lead to a plethora of escapist entertainment. Sophisticates were in vogue, on the silver screen that is.

Mae Clarke and Boris Karloff in *Frankenstein*

Nick and Nora Charles would begin their detecting career in *The Thin Man*, *Snow White* would capture the hearts of America, John Wayne would begin his domination of the Old West and Shirley Temple, the tiniest of the Fox blondes, would become a box office champ. Marlene Dietrich would slink her way through many a classic, Tarzan and his mate would swing across the theater screens, Mae West, with a twinkle in her eye, would invite audiences to come up and see her sometime, Fred and Ginger would dance their way into film history, Jean Harlow was the blonde bombshell, Bette Davis was a *Marked Woman*, Garbo talked, and laughed, and fell in love.

Laurel and Hardy inspired zany mayhem, Errol Flynn would swashbuckle his way into female affections and 1939 would present a film list that even today sends film buffs into a state of nirvana: *Gone With the Wind, The Wizard of Oz, Son of Frankenstein, Stagecoach, Ninotchka, Dark Victory, Destry Rides Again, Goodbye, Mr. Chips, The Little Princess, The Hunchback of*

Miriam Hopkins and Fredric March in *Dr. Jekyll and Mr. Hyde*

Notre Dame, Mr. Smith Goes to Washington, Gunga Din, Love Affair and *Wuthering Heights*. And then there was Universal—a Mecca to horror film fans. Universal made Hollywood history with legendary bogeyman Bela Lugosi as *Dracula* and then followed that amazing feat by introducing Boris Karloff in *Frankenstein*. The studio would dominate the horror field until doing a fast fade in the 1940s, but until that time they delighted, frightened and swept audiences away from the terror of reality. The gruesome twosome of *Dracula* and *Frankenstein* would be followed by such glorious gems as *Murders in the Rue Morgue* and *The Mummy* (1932), *The Invisible Man* (1933), *The Black Cat* (1934), *The Raven, Werewolf of London* and *Bride of Frankenstein* (1935), *The Invisible Ray, Dracula's Daughter* (1936) and *Son of Frankenstein* (1939).

Universal's success did not go unnoticed by the other majors. They contributed their own classics to horror film anuals: Paramount delved into the decadent side of humanity in *Dr. Jekyll and Mr. Hyde* (1932), *Supernatural* (1933), *Island of Lost Souls* (1933) and the sadistic *Murders in the Zoo* (1933). RKO would weigh in with *King Kong* (1933) and *The Most Dangerous Game* (1932); Warner Bros. would wax poetic in *Mystery of the Wax Museum* (1933) and MGM would tap their maver-

The Wicked Witch (Margaret Hamilton) spies on Dorothy Gale (Judy Garland) in *The Wizard of Oz.*

ick filmmakers to bring us *The Mask of Fu Manchu* (1932), *Freaks* (1932), *Mark of the Vampire* (1935) and *Mad Love* (1935).

Universal heroines were standard issue—lovely delicate flowers terrified by monsters and rescued by manly protectors who would sweep them off their feet and take them away from all this terror. But the '30s also provided three of my favorite over-the-top examples of femininity, one feisty heroine (Glenda Farrell), one deliciously decadent nymphomaniac (Myrna Loy) and one adventurous little girl (Judy Garland).

Dorothy Gale (Judy Garland) in *The Wizard of Oz* has always been every little girl's favorite heroine. She faces mean old Miss Gulch (Margaret Hamilton) when Gulch tries to take Toto away ("You go away or I'll bite you myself, you wicked old witch!"). She slaps the lion on his snout when he threatens Toto (even before realizing he was a *cowardly* lion), and she leads her friends to the Witch's castle to retrieve the wicked old Witch's broomstick. We all shivered in our pj's as the Wicked Witch

Fay Wray and Glenda Farrell in *Mystery of the Wax Museum*

threatened Dorothy in the Munchkinland square and gasped when she wrote, "SURRENDER DOROTHY" in the skies above the Emerald City. We hid our little moppet heads as the monkeys carried Dorothy through the skies to the castle and we cried as Dorothy said good-bye to the Scarecrow. Every little girl wanted to *be* Dorothy and travel over the rainbow, and now as adults we still dream about it. However, the real star was the wonderful Margaret Hamilton as The Wicked Witch of the West. She cackled wildly, frightened little children and small animals, and sent chills down our spines with every crack of her tongue ("I'll get you, and your little dog too!"). A simply sublime witch.

Mystery of the Wax Museum advertises Fay Wray and Lionel Atwill as its stars. But it is Glenda Farrell who steals the show, managing to hold her own with the flamboyant Atwill. Farrell would make her mark as a tough-talking blonde in the Jean Harlow mold. Before appearing in *Wax Museum* she had appeared in *I Am a Fugitive from a Chain Gang* and *Little Caesar*. The wise-cracking blonde would come into her own with the Torchy Blane series in 1938.

Glenda Farrell steals the show as Florence Dempsey in *Mystery of the Wax Museum.*

Farrell portrays mouthy reporter Florence Dempsey, roommate of the dull Charlotte Duncan (Wray). As Florence makes fun of Charlotte's boyfriend, she is chided for her frivolous ways. Florence embraces life while Charlotte hides behind it.

Charlotte: "I don't think you could have a real affair. I don't think you could care for anyone."

Florence: "I've been in love so many times my heart's callused. But I never hit one with dough. I'd rather die with an apoplectic heart from shaking cocktails and bankers than expire in a pan of dirty dishwater."

Lionel Atwill, as the demented Ivan Igor, has been masterminding the theft of bodies and using them to restock his wax museum. When Charlotte visits her artist boyfriend at the studio, Florence discovers an amazing resemblance between Joan of Arc and a missing body. She rushes to her newspaper office where she engages in snappy patter with her despised editor, Jim (Frank McHugh).

Florence: "Hello, light of my life."

Jim: "Well, well, Prussic Acid."

Florence, visiting the exhibit with Charlotte, sneaks over to the Joan of Arc and scrapes a bit of wax from her foot, then follows a henchman of Igor's to a deserted basement. She's accompanied by a rich young man, Winton (Gavin Gordon), she met the night before in the slammer. He is a little hesitant to get involved, having had enough interaction with the police. "OK, brother, then you can go to some nice warm place and I don't mean California." Florence climbs in a basement window and explores the area, scaring herself as she bumps into things. Unfortunately, Florence is not only adventurous, she tends to jump to conclusions, notably when she calls the cops—convinced a body is in an oblong box she has discovered. The police burst into the room and approach the box with trepidation; however, it's not a murderer who inhabits the house, but bootleggers. Florence grabs a couple bottles as they leave.

In the car Winton professes his love for the daring Florence.

Winton: "I've only known you for 24 hours but I'm in love with you."

Florence: "It doesn't usually take that long."

Florence heads back to the newspaper office where she tackles her considerably unhappy editor.

Florence: "Mitt me kid, I got a classic."

Jim: "...an evil spirit to mar my happiness."

Florence heads back to the museum where she is just in time to save the wretched Charlotte from a wax bath. Actually, she sensibly runs screaming for the police—a nice touch—rather than stay and put her pretty neck in jeopardy; she actually uses her head for something other than a hat rack.

Florence returns to the newsroom in glory, jovially accepting congratulations from her colleagues.

Florence: "Well, how about it, poison ivy?"

Jim: "Rotten. You had a million dollars worth of luck with you."

Florence: "Could I possibly do anything that would meet with your approval?"

Jim: "Yeah. Cut out this crazy business, act like a lady, marry me."

Florence: "I'm gonna get even with you, you dirty stiff. I'll do it."

Will they live happily ever after? Maybe; however, we all know

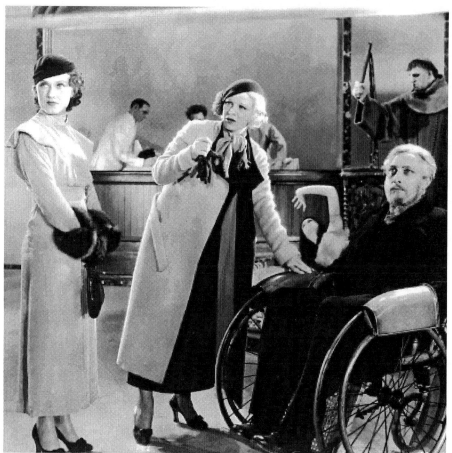

Fay and Glenda meet up with Lionel Atwill in *Mystery of the Wax Museum*.

she'll be back in the newsroom before the honeymoon's over. And we're glad.

Farrell spiels forth her newswoman patter with the zeal of an early Rosalind Russell and is a welcome change from your comparable '30s scream queens.

Myrna Loy. Her name brings to mind the shaking of a cocktail mixer from *The Thin Man* or the aroma of fresh baked apple pie from *The Best Years of Our Lives*. But Loy, under contract to Warners, began her career playing mysterious Oriental women in *Crimson City* (1928) followed a year later with *The Desert Song*. She would eventually sign with MGM where she would enact her last Oriental role as the misanthropic sex-fiend Fah Lo See, daughter of Fu Manchu (Boris Karloff), in *The Mask of Fu Manchu*.

Myrna Loy in *The Mask of Fu Manchu*

Much has been written about this campy delight, but this all-star queen of evilness is one of the highlights of this chapter. Every line she utters is dripping with honey-coated daggers (screenwriters Irene Kuhn, Edgar Allan Woolf and John Willard must have chuckled with wicked glee while composing the dialogue). Loy's eyes brim with a silent mirth as she doles out Fah's vicious tortures and ludicrous speeches.

Fu Manchu is desperately seeking the sword and mask of Genghis Khan, which will give him the power to control the world! He kidnaps Dr. Barton (Lawrence Grant) who was to head the expedition. Fu calls Fah into the throne room. "My daughter, explain to this gentleman the rewards that might be his. Point out to him the delights of our lovely county, the promise of our beautiful women—even my daughter, even *that* for you." Loy manages to maintain a blank look on her face while Karloff delights in delivering his over-dramatic lines with gusto.

Barton does not know the location of the artifacts and Fu holds him for ransom. The sword and mask are delivered by the virile Terrence Granville (Charles Starrett), true love of Grant's virtuous daughter. As Granville confidently strides into the throne room, Fah smiles and catches her breath. When he removes the "sword" she again catches her breath and parts her hands in delight. Unfortunately for Granville, the sword is a fake. As he is led away Fah smiles with enjoyment.

As Granville hangs by his hands Fah watches as his shirt is torn off. "The whip!" she yells. She watches in orgasmic ecstasy as they beat Granville, yelling "Faster, faster, faster, faster, faster!" Subtle? Not in the least, but perversely entertaining nonetheless.

Granville is taken to Fah's rooms and placed on a divan. She leans down to kiss him as her father enters. She looks up with a smile, leering, "He is not entirely unhandsome, is he my father?"

"For a white man, no. May I suggest, however, a slight delay in your customary procedure."

"You have further need of him?"

"I have. He shall still be the means of discovering for me where they have hidden the sword and mask."

"And for that purpose you will..." Fah asks, leaning forward in excitement.

"Precisely." Karloff lisps.

We're not sure exactly what Fu is going to do to Granville, be we know it's going to be nasty.

Loy has no more amusing dialogue and disappears from the finale all together. Perhaps they were saving her for a sequel that never came about.

Like the thoroughly evil villainesses of Disney, Fah has no redeeming values—and that's why we love her.

"What I like about you is you're rock bottom... It's a great comfort for
a girl to know she could not possibly sink any lower."
—*The Big Steal*, 1949

"You know how to whistle, don't you Steve? You just put your lips
together and blow."—*To Have and Have Not*, 1944

"Doesn't it ever enter a man's head that a
woman can do without him?"
—*Road House*, 1948

"Men like to see women cry. It makes them feel superior."
—*The Spiral Staircase*, 1946

The 1940s. The men were overseas, women were working in factories and children huddled by heat registers during air-raid drills. Teenagers would visit the local cinemas to watch John Wayne and Gary Cooper shoot 'em up, Humphrey Bogart chase the stuff that dreams are made of and Judy Garland, Gene Kelly and Fred Astaire make movie magic in

Kent Smith, Simone Simon and Jane Randolph in *The Cat People*

MGM's glorious musicals. Screwball comedies reached their peak in the 1940s with films such as *The Philadelphia Story, My Favorite Wife* and *His Girl Friday*. Hope and Crosby were on the road, Abbott and Costello joined the cinematic army, Orson Welles was obsessing over Rosebud, Jimmy Stewart was having a wonderful life and Humphrey Bogart opened Rick's Place. Radio shows were the entertainment of the average folks, who never missed Jack Benny and *The Shadow*. With men off to war, women were taking charge of their homes, their families, and their new-found responsibilities in the war factories.

The tough-talking dame would become a staple of an emerging film genre, noir. The men were scoundrels or easy pickings, the women cheap floozies looking for an easy ride to the good life. Hollywood actresses were in their glory, as prime parts for women became standard operating procedure. Veronica Lake, Lauren Bacall, Lizabeth Scott and Barbara Stanwyck would become the beneficiaries of this dark trend.

Jane Randolph and Ann Carter in *The Curse of the Cat People*

Universal horror films were on a downward spiral, their crown as king of horror passing on to the unpretentious and unsuspecting RKO, whose resident geniuses—producer Val Lewton and directors Robert Wise, Jacques Tourneur and Mark Robson would almost single-handedly save the struggling genre.

Other than the intelligently drawn Lewton heroines, horror didn't offer much to actresses during this war-ravaged decade. Jane Randolph had the difficult task of portraying the other woman in Jacques Tourneur's *Cat People* (1942) from RKO. Alice unwillingly falls in love with the married Oliver (Kent Smith), who is miserable in his unconsummated marriage to Irena (Simone Simon). Alice faces the most famous Lewton "bus" as she is terrorized in the swimming pool and then flees into the street only to be startled (as is the audience) by the air brakes of a bus. Unfortunately, Randolph's performance is constantly overlooked due to the flamboyant Simon character. Randolph would return in *The Curse of the Cat People* as the mother of sad and misunderstood Amy (Ann

Christine Gordon and Frances Dee in *I Walked with a Zombie*

Carter). Another Lewton heroine, Frances Dee as Betsy in *I Walked with a Zombie*, also falls in love with a married man, this one the husband of her zombified patient. She faces strange terrors as she takes a horror-filled Lewton walk through the swamp trying to help the unfortunate Jessica (Christine Gordon).

Louise Allbritton, as the scheming Katherine Caldwell, sets out to destroy Dracula, while acquiring his powers and immortality in *Son of Dracula*. Allbritton is chilling as an evil woman, who will stop at nothing, including the destruction of her family, to attain her desires.

Louise Allbritton in *Son of Dracula*

Femme fatale Gale Sondergaard would have a feline field day as the sly Tylette, Shirley Temple's conniving cat in *The Blue Bird* (1940) and as Sherlock Holmes nemesis in *The Spider Woman* (1944).

Holmes: "...Something uncanny about it, something monstrous and horrible. Something that drives these poor fellows to their so-called suicides... murders brilliantly conceived and executed. They're very near to being perfect crimes. Indubitably these murders are the work of a well-organized gang and directing them is one of the most fiendishly clever minds in Europe today. I suspect a woman... Because the method is peculiarly subtle and cruel. Feline, not Canine... the bloke is driven to suicide and in that case it's murder."

Watson: "Driven. That sounds like a woman doesn't it?"

The Spider Woman and Holmes verbally fence using the "I knew that you knew that I knew" routine. The best bit in the film has the notorious Spider Woman visit Holmes at 221B Baker Street with her young nephew. The kid is worth the price of admission for his hysterical imitation of a miniature Dwight Frye as he hops around catching flies.

As the 1950s approached, the survivors were home from the real horrors of the battlefield, women were safely ensconced in their kitchens once more, horror films were dead and science fiction films would dominate the next decade.

Basil Rathbone, Gale Sondergaard and Nigel Bruce in *Spider Woman*

"CRIMES OF PASSION PENT UP IN HIS SAVAGE HEART!"
—Creature from the Black Lagoon, 1954

"A Beautiful Woman by Day—A Lusting Queen Wasp by Night."
—The Wasp Woman, 1959

"Mankind's first fantastic flight to VENUS—The Female Planet!"
—Queen of Outer Space, 1958

1950s. The black and white flickering of the tiny round television screen hypnotized a nation. Families lined up on the sofa to laugh with Uncle Miltie, Red Buttons, Amos 'n' Andy, Our Miss Brooks, Jack Benny, Red Skelton, Jackie Gleason and George Gobel. They waited eagerly for *Texaco Star Theater* on NBC as well as *Your Show of Shows, I Love Lucy, You Bet Your Life, Disneyland, The $64,000 Question, The Ed Sullivan Show, Gunsmoke, Wagon Train, Have Gun Will Travel* and *The Rifleman*. Forties' teens were now heading to a place called Korea for a

SEE
the nerve-shattering
Dance of Death!

SEE
the Woman Eater
ensnare the beauties
of two continents!

SEE
its hideous arms
devour them in a
death-embrace!

GEORGE COULOURIS
VERA DAY
is
The Woman Eater

Written by BRANDON FLEMING · Produced by GUIDO CORN
Directed by CHARLES SAUNDERS · A FORTRESS FILM PRODUCTION
A COLUMBIA PICTURES RELEASE

war they didn't understand, while at home family values reigned supreme.

In a rush to decrease their huge star salaries, Hollywood studio moguls brushed aside major stars like annoying dandruff. The studio system was dead and a decline could be seen in the Hollywood product. The studios frantically scrambled for gimmicks to combat the new technology of television. Glorious Technicolor, breathtaking Cinemascope and Stereophonic sound along with Amazing 3-D were just a few rabbits pulled out of Hollywood's brown derby.

Bette Davis fastened her seat belt for a bumpy ride, Judy Garland was reborn as a star, Judy Holliday was *Born Yesterday*, Gloria Swanson was ready for her close-up, John Wayne was *The Quiet Man*, Spencer Tracy had a *Bad Day at Black Rock*, David Niven went *Around the World in 80 Days*, Maurice Chevalier was thanking heaven for little girls, Susan Hayward wanted to live and Marilyn Monroe got serious at the *Bus Stop*.

Families, looking for cheap entertainment for the kiddies, packed some Kool-Aid and popcorn, put the kids in their jammies and headed for the local drive-in. Teenagers, looking for a little make-out time, headed there for the same reason or to the local drive-in restaurant for burgers, fries, and shakes.

Independent studios cranked out product for this new audience of fans who were more interested in the drive-in experience than in the movies shown—and society's new-found fear of technology made science fiction films a perfect exploitative choice. Since women were back home where they supposedly belonged, the tough dames of the 1940s did a quick fade and Suzy homemaker took her place.

THE MONSTER CREATED BY ATOMS GONE WILD!

20. Century-Fox presents

The FLY

AL HEDISON · PATRICIA OWENS · VINCENT PRICE · HERBERT MARSHALL

KURT NEUMANN JAMES CLAVELL in CINEMASCOPE and TERROR-COLOR by DE LUXE!

Women did boldly go where no woman had gone before—outer space, but unfortunately they were just along for the ride, although they sure brewed a mean cup of coffee. They also appeared as sexy aliens in a list of *non*-Academy Award contenders such as *Cat-Women of the Moon, Fire Maidens of Outer Space, Devil Girl from Mars* and *Queen of Outer Space* starring that well-known thesp, Zsa Zsa Gabor.

The Fly (1958) was a notable exception to the rule as Patricia Owens turns in a thoughtful performance as the wife of a scientist who manages to turn himself into an overgrown insect. Owens bravely destroys her creepy-crawler husband in a printing press before being arrested for his murder. Positively one of the most original sci-fi films of the decade with a great female lead role.

She Devil (1957), a not-so-great film but a drive-in delight, has one of the bitchiest women this side of PMSville. Mari Blanchard stars in this overly talkie sci-fi/horror yarn as a destitute dying woman who is given a new serum by a duo of kindly scientists. Miraculously, the serum saves her life and in the process makes her indestructible—she's even able to change her hair color at will, which comes in handy as she

FEMALE MONSTER!

THEY CREATED AN INHUMAN BEING WHO DESTROYED EVERYTHING SHE TOUCHED!

SHE DEVIL

The woman they couldn't kill!

starring MARI BLANCHARD

JACK KELLY · ALBERT DEKKER

Featuring JOHN ARCHER · FAY BAKER · BLOSSOM ROCK · PAUL CAVANAGH

Produced and Directed by KURT NEUMANN

Screenplay by CARROLL YOUNG and KURT NEUMANN

Story "The Adaptive Ultimate" by JOHN JESSEL

A REGALSCOPE PICTURE

A REGAL FILMS, INC. PRODUCTION · Released by 20th CENTURY-FOX

sets out to get everything she's always wanted and woe to anyone who stands in her way. Needing new clothes, she whacks some poor schnook over the head with a glass ashtray in a ritzy clothing store, hides in a dressing room, her hair turns blonde, and she merrily saunters out, free as a bird—*vulture* that is. Kyra (Blanchard) seduces gullible scientist Dr. Scott (Jack Kelly), convincing him not to search for an antidote, then decides she wants to marry an obnoxious millionaire; she strangles his wife (in her brunette disguise), marries the dolt, and then kills him by forcing their car over a

cliff. Of course, she emerges from the wreckage little the worse for wear. Dr. Scott and Dr. Bach (Albert Dekker) knock her unconscious by using carbon monoxide and then operate, turning her back into the pathetic creature she once was. Of course, during those days the murderess could not be allowed to survive, and Kyra promptly returns to her previous condition and dies of tuberculosis.

Patricia Neal managed to control Gort in *The Day the Earth Stood Still* (1951) but, for the most part, women were relegated to the background, providing enough screams and sex appeal for 1950s audiences. There was one place women dominated—poster art for the 1950s sci-fi posters. No self-respecting poster debuted without some scantily clad babe being carried away by a hulking monster.

Jane Fonda as *Barbarella*

"Who gives up the pill? Who takes sex to outer space?
Who's the girl of the 21st Century?
Who nearly dies of pleasure?"
—*Barbarella*, 1968

The 1960s. Was there ever a more bizarre decade of American history? Mini-dresses and go-go boots were the rage. Kids tuned out and turned on, Vietnam was a stone around everyone's neck, and movies left behind the innocence of the past. Families were still hypnotized by the flickering tube and spent quality time together watching *The Real McCoys, Bonanza, Hazel, Candid Camera* and *The Dick Van Dyke Show.*

At the movies Shirley MacLaine visited *The Apartment*, Shirley Jones seduced *Elmer Gantry*, Paul Newman was *The Hustler*, Natalie Wood and Warren Beatty enjoyed a little *Splendor in the Grass*, Mrs. Robinson put the moves on Dustin Hoffman, Rosemary had a baby and William Holden rode with the *Wild Bunch*... It was truly a *Mad Mad Mad Mad*

World. Hip British comedies were the rage, but like modern art, nobody really understood them—but everyone pretended to, while in the U.S. Peter Sellers confounded audiences in *Dr. Strangelove.*

Horror films took a decidedly grisly turn with the mother-obsessed Norman Bates in *Psycho*, the wacko Bette Davis in *What Ever Happened to Baby Jane?*, the flesh-eating zombies from *Night of the Living Dead*, the pre-slasher slasher flicks *Homicidal, Strait-Jacket* and *Repulsion*— and the putridly disgusting *Blood Feast.* Sci-fi went big-budget with

the A productions *2001: A Space Odyssey* and *Planet of the Apes.*

Women's roles weren't even as good as they had been in the 1950s, for now horror displayed a truly nasty side as women became victims of

axes, knives and psychos, or were cast as bimbos providing handy diversions for James Bond. The queen of the 1960s scream queens was without a doubt *Barbarella* (1967). Jane Fonda and then-husband Roger Vadim are responsible for this adaptation of a hip French comic... like much of the 1960s, the film makes little sense and failed to rocket Fonda to the sex kitten fame Vadim was seeking for her. Thankfully Fonda had talent and managed to put this turkey in her past and sink her teeth into some real roles rather than the outer space hunks she met up with in *Barbarella.* One exception to the nymphet 1960s was the

Mexican film *Wrestling Women vs. the Aztec Mummy* (1964). Two wrestling Amazon beauties, Loretta Venus and The Golden Ruby, help an

Tim Curry is Frank-N-Furter in *The Rocky Horror Picture Show*

archeologist battle an evil Oriental mastermind, the Black Dragon, and after he is done away with by the mummy, they take on the dusty old fiend himself. Use the fast forward button on your VCR to skip everything but the women's fight scenes. They're great as the wrestling Amazons take on gangs of thugs, beating them to a pulp again and again and again. The follow-up is *Wrestling Women vs. the Aztec Ape*. The 1970s were quickly approaching, although most aging hippies failed to notice. The mid-1970s would provide a bizarre alien bitch whose amazing cult following will never fade—yes, I'm speaking about Frank-n-Furter the bitchy, decadent, perverse, murdering mad doctor from *The Rocky Horror Picture Show* (1975). While technically not a woman, Frank is absolutely a queen bitch of the universe as he slinks about in his black corset and fishnet stockings—"I've been making a man, with blond hair and a tan, and he's good for relieving my tension; I'm just a sweet transvestite from transsexual Transylvania." Tim Curry as Frank simpers, seduces and shocks as he cavorts through this perverse tribute to horror films. As his world crumbles about him, he pathetically proclaims, "It's not easy having a good time."

"A NEW HOPE"—*Star Wars*, 1977

"In space no one can hear you scream."—*Alien,* 1979

"Be afraid. Be very afraid."—*The Fly*, 1986

It was the best of times, it was the worst of times. Television really was becoming the "boob tube," music was bland and films were dark and depressing or on the flip side, fluffy and moronic. These are the decades of alternate universes. In one ghastly universe, women were dragged kicking and screaming into the gory 1970s, '80s and '90s. In the other universe women became the heroes, fighting side by side with men for truth, justice and the Galactic way. These intrepid women fiercely waged battles with evil dark forces, bloodthirsty vampires, chest-bursting aliens, robots from the future, flesh-eating zombies and even the evilest villains of them all–Nazis. They are the typical Hitchcock hero, regular gals placed in extraordinary circumstances, who manage to survive their incredible journey.

The first universe is inhabited by psycho slashers who prey mainly on teenagers, preferring nubile young ladies, especially the promiscuous ones. The virgin always manages to survive. The sexual liberation of the 1960s never seemed to have an effect on horror filmmakers, who chose to have their heroine/victims remain pristine examples of purity. An archaic attitude obvious to almost everyone except said filmmakers and some Republicans.

Any geek with a video camera began to make movies featuring inane scripts, horribly bad acting, gratuitous T&A and eager actress wannabes,

Peter Cushing, Carrie Fisher and David Prowse in *Star Wars*

who happily remove their clothes at the drop of a clapper. Women were chainsawed, dismembered, terrorized, brutally raped, butchered and mangled. We prayed the psycho would finally do in that annoying screaming girl in *Texas Chain Saw Massacre*, grew disgusted with the sequelitis and resurrection of fiends from Jason to the Shape, and don't even get me started on Freddy, whose bloody antics forced me to leave the theater. *Re-Animator* repulsed women with its gross sex scene between a restrained woman and a decapitated head. Please people, let's show *some* restraint. This universe deserves to be swallowed by a black hole and bloodily spit out on the other side of the galaxy.

The other universe is the meat and potatoes of this chapter. In 1977, a long time ago in a galaxy far, far away, a Star Destroyer majestically flew across theater screens. Audiences gasped and cinematic history was made by George Lucas, a weird assortment of aliens, a crack special effects team and a relatively unknown cast consisting of the naive Luke Skywalker (Mark Hamill), the dashing Han Solo (Harrison Ford) and the feisty Princess Leia Organa (Carrie Fisher). *STAR WARS*. Even today when the first note of the Academy Award-winning score (by John

Princess Leia places the Death Star plans in R2D2 in *Star Wars*.

Williams) sounds, my heart beats a little faster and I begin to feel the same adrenaline rush I felt back in 1977. Forget Dorothy and Oz, I wanted to *be* Princess Leia, fighting to save the galaxy from the evil Darth Vader and the Empire. Being chased by Harrison Ford wouldn't be bad either.

For anyone living in a cave, the Galaxy is ruled by the evil Empire who are building a giant Death Star they plan to use to finally defeat the rebel alliance. Young Luke Skywalker and his mentor Obi Wan Kenobi along with pilot Han Solo and Chewbacca set out to return a set of plans for the Death Star to Princess Leia. Leia has been captured by Darth Vader.

Leia is one tough cookie as she is taken before Grand Moff Tarkin (Peter Cushing). Six hefty stormtroopers surround the diminutive Princess as she confronts Vader.

"Governor Tarkin. I should have expected to find you holding Vader's leash. I recognized your foul stench when I was brought on board."

"Charming to the last."

The Princess is rescued by Luke and Han, sort of. She ends up doing most of the rescuing as she grabs a blaster from Han and fires into a wall ordering Han, "Into the garbage chute, fly boy."

Luke is smitten with the Princess, but then so is Han. "I'm either going to kill her or I'm starting to like her."

Leia, Luke and Han escape and lead the rebels in a successful attack on the Death Star.

On the *Star Wars Trilogy* deluxe laser disc box set, George Lucas discusses the casting of Princess Leia: "I wanted somebody teenager-like. So it was finding somebody who could hold their own against strong actors and still be the Princess that she needed to be and still be the authority figure she needed to be, and make her believable."

Princess Leia gave little girls a much-needed role model, a strong independent woman willing to risk everything to save her people, but also a woman who remained focused but feminine to the last (throughout *Star Wars* she is clad in flowing white robes showcasing her innocence, but her attire would change throughout the series as her character matured—notably ending with the eye-popping slave girl costume, which even became the focus of a *Friends* episode).

The Empire Strikes Back (1980) and the Princess is right in the midst of the battle, commanding troops, bantering with Han Solo, and escaping the evil Vader in the City in the Clouds.

The sexual electricity between Leia and Han heats up to boiling as their delightful repartee provides a welcome relief from the darkness encompassing the sequel to *Star Wars*. They are a cosmic Tracy and Hepburn as they bicker their way across the galaxy.

The rebels, based on the ice planet Hoth, are under attack from the Empire. They are preparing to abandon the planet. Han and Leia argue about Han's plan to leave.

"Han."

"Yes your highness."

"I thought you had decided to stay. Han, we need you."

"We need?"

"Yes."

"What about *you* need?"

Princess Leia and Luke (Mark Hamill) escape Jaba the Hutt in *The Return of the Jedi*.

"*I need*? I don't know what you're talking about."

"You probably don't. ...Afraid I was going the leave without giving you a good-bye kiss?"

"I'd just as soon kiss a wookie!"

"I can arrange that."

Lucas has long taken hits for his flat dialogue, but romance-starved teen girls weren't complaining.

Leia must be pulled from the command station as the Stormtroopers break through. Han, Chewy, C3PO and Leia escape on the *Millennium Falcon*, evading a star destroyer in an asteroid field. As they make repairs, Han tries once again to break through Leia's tough exterior.

"Come on, admit it. Sometimes you think I'm all right."

"Occasionally. Maybe. When you're not acting like a scoundrel."

"Scoundrel! Scoundrel. I like the sound of that... there aren't enough scoundrels in your life."

"I happen to like nice men."

"I'm a nice man."

Leia, along with most female audience members, is melting fast. But she never lets her guard down enough to allow love to interfere with her main goal of defeating the Empire.

Leia, Han and Chewy are captured by the Empire in the City in the Clouds and tortured. They are being used as bait to lure Luke to a confrontation with Darth Vader. Han is frozen in carbonite and given to Boba Fett, the bounty hunter. Their good-bye kiss in a orange backlit scene is worthy of *Gone With the Wind*. As Han is lowered into the freezing chamber, Leia proclaims, "I love you." "I know." Leia and Chewy are on their way to Vader's ship when they escape, but it is too late to save Han. As they take off Leia hears Luke calling to her and they race back, barely in time to save him.

1983 saw *The Return of the Jedi*. Leia, masquerading as a bounty hunter, leads Chewy into the nefarious den of Jabba the Hutt, a huge slug-like creature who proudly displays the frozen Han Solo on his wall. As Leia releases Han from the Carbonite, they are discovered. Han is thrown into a dungeon and Leia is made a slave of Jabba wearing the tiniest of slave girl costumes. My, she had matured. Luke shows up, they all escape and lead an attack to shut down a force field protecting the new death star which is orbiting the forest moon of Endor, a planet inhabited by a cuddly race of little bear-like creatures. The rebels are having a difficult time keeping the Stormtroopers at bay while trying to enter the fortress controlling the force field. Leia, covering Han as he tries to hot-wire the door, is hit in the shoulder by a laser blast. They are trapped and ordered to surrender by the Stormtroopers. Leia secretly shows Han a blaster she is holding. "I love you," he says with relief. "I know," she answers.

Of course the Empire is destroyed thanks to Luke and his converted father, Darth Vader. Everybody lives happily ever after.

Princess Leia would pave the way for a new cinematic heroine. No longer would women be plot devices or lovely victims of monsters. They were the focal point of some of the largest money-making films of all time. Princess Leia toppled more than one empire.

Sigourney Weaver as Ripley in *Alien*

Star Wars would be followed the next year by *Superman* (1978) starring Christopher Reeve and Margot Kidder as Lois Lane. The Lois Lane character has always been annoying, especially so in this adaptation. Lois Lane never manages realistically to carry off the strong woman guise, perhaps because she is always involved in stupidly dangerous stunts, forcing Superman to spend most of his valuable time rescuing her.

In 1979 the U.S. was invaded by *Alien* as the grizzled and weary crew of the freighter *Nostromo* return to Earth with a valuable cargo. Virtually a remake of *It! The Terror from Beyond Space*, both films had two female crew members but the women onboard the *Nostromo* were not the "get me a cup of coffee" type of gals. Lambert (Veronica Cartwright) was a whiny complainer, and when cited for it, she replies, "I like to complain." Ripley (Sigourney Weaver) is the third in command and refuses to unquarantine Dallas, Lambert and Kane when they try to re-enter the ship after Kane is attacked by the mysterious egg creature. Android Ash (Ian Holm) disobeys her and opens the door.

Ripley is a woman of many talents: she knows the ship backward and forward, is a pilot and has no qualms about taking charge after Dallas disappears.

Rapidly losing crew members to the deadly alien, Ripley decides on a drastic course of action. "We're going to blow up the ship. We'll take our chances in the shuttle." The only chink in Ripley's armor is the cat that accompanies the crew. The three remaining members split up. Ripley hears screaming and rushes toward the sound, Lambert and Parker (Yaphet Kotto) have both become victims of the alien. Ripley sets

the self-destruct activator and enters the shuttle. The alien, realizing her plan, blocks the door of the shuttle. Ripley rushes back to try to stop the self-destruct but is too late. She screams at the computer (which the crew called Mother): "You bitch!"

Ripley takes a flame-thrower and heads back toward the shuttle. The alien is nowhere to be found. She straps in, having only seconds to get out of there before the ship blows. "I got you, you son of a bitch." Of course, it wasn't quite that easy. The alien is on the shuttle. Ripley manages to put on a spacesuit and blow the bastard into space.

Leia led the way—but Ripley was the real queen bitch of outer space. The idea of a woman surviving—let alone destroying the monster herself—with no help from anyone (re: men) was a refreshing concept whose time had come. Audiences were amazed and astounded, and loved it, propelling *Alien* to a coveted position as a top moneymaker for 1979.

Ripley becomes a surrogate mother to Newt in *Aliens*.

Alien had no romance, no sex, no beauty. It was a down and dirty adventure film that took no liberties with its female characters (except for the tiny underwear Weaver wore in the film—how anybody could do any actual work in those things is anybody's guess).

Outside of *Star Wars,* most sequels are emphatically inferior to the original film. *Aliens'* (1986) director James Cameron had his hands full when the studio decided to visit a planet full of the viciously intelligent aliens. Cameron is one of today's hottest directors, a director who has a remarkable track record when it comes to female characters. Perhaps he was influenced by producer (and wife at the time) Gale Anne Hurd. *Aliens* develops Ripley as a heartbreakingly complex character who sadly regrets leaving behind a child on Earth while she worked in space.

Found floating in space 57 years after winning her battle with the alien, things are not all sugar and spice for Ripley. The Company, unhappy she blew up a 42 million dollar ship, declares her unfit to hold a license as a commercial flight officer. She is released , but on probation. Ripley is forced to work on a loading dock. Until... The Company has sent teraformers to planet LV426, the home of the face-hugging alien monsters. There has been no communication from the settlers and the

Ripley and Newt discover the egg chamber in *Aliens*.

Company approaches Ripley to go with a squad of Marines to find out what happened. She refuses, but cannot live with the nightmares that haunt her, so she finally agrees.

The Marines are some tough hombres and they are loaded for bear. The squad has its share of women, notably Vasquez (Jenette Goldstein) who makes Ripley look like Shirley Temple.

The Marines find no one alive except a terrified little girl, Newt (Carrie Henn), who is drawn to Ripley. Ripley becomes a mother figure to Newt, a much-needed sign of humanity in the hard-as-nails character. When the Marines stumble into the lair of the aliens, the slaughter is wholesale. The green commander Lt. Gorman (William Hope) falls apart and Ripley must drive to the regiment's rescue. The most frightening plotline of *Aliens* is the failure of the Marines. The idea that this superior fighting group that we all rely upon, cannot defeat the aliens is terrifying, forcing the audience to face the conclusion there may be no hope. The remaining Marines shakily plot a course of action.

Ripley: "I say we take off and nuke the entire site from orbit."

Burke: "This installation has a substantial dollar value attached to it."

Ripley: "They can bill me."

The rag-tag band tries to escape, Vasquez bringing up the rear. She is trapped by an alien and shoots it in the head. The creature's acid-blood splatters over her. Lt. Gorman goes back for Vasquez and, when trapped, sets off a grenade; Vasquez clutches his hand before the explosion. Meanwhile, Newt has been taken by an alien.

Ripley, Cpl. Hicks (Michael Biehn) and Bishop (Lance Henriksen) reach the shuttle. Ripley duct tapes (the best invention since sliced bread) two weapons together and has 19 minutes to find Newt before the entire complex explodes.

Newt, in the alien's lair and partially cocooned, cries out for Ripley. Ripley grabs Newt and runs right into the nastiest mother in the universe, the alien Queen. Making it clear she will torch the eggs, the alien allows Ripley and Newt to back out of the lair. Giving the creature an "I lied" look, Ripley turns the flame-thrower on the eggs. The shuttle reaches the safety of the ship orbiting the planet, but their worries are not over—the Queen has gotten a free ride on the shuttle and is mighty annoyed with Ripley.

Ripley climbs into a cargo mover and the two very pissed off mothers battle to the death. Eventually Ripley manages to maneuver the alien into outer space. Weaver was nominated for an Academy Award for her portrayal of Ripley.

Ripley is more ferocious in this film, but any mother will turn into a beast when protecting her child, in this case Newt.

The follow-up, *Alien 3*, totally alienated audiences in the first five minutes when scripters killed off Hicks and Newt before the story even began. And then they killed off Ripley! Talk about ticked off patrons.

Returning to the past, 1936 to be exact, George Lucas, Steven Spielberg and Karen Allen brought Marion Ravenwood to vivid life in

Marion (Karen Allen) is on the adventure of her life in *Raiders of the Lost Ark*.

Raiders of the Lost Ark (1981). A decidedly updated version of the serial heroine, Marion doesn't take crap from *anybody*.

Indiana Jones (Harrison Ford), seeking a medallion owned by Prof. Ravenwood, travels to Nepal where he finds Marion, Ravenwood's daughter, who has just completed a shot drinking contest with the locals—she's still standing but you should see the other guy.

"Indiana Jones. I always knew someday you'd come walking back through my door. I never doubted that. Something made it inevitable. So what are you doing here in Nepal?"

When he starts to answer she hauls off and gives him a right to the jaw. Their previous relationship didn't exactly end on a happy note.

Nazis show up, Jones and Marion desperately fight for their lives. Marion takes a break from the frenzy of battle to gulp from a stream of whisky flowing from a bullet-riddled barrel before conking a bad guy over the head. As the villains run for the hills and her bar burns to the ground, she picks herself up commenting, "Well, Jones, you still haven't forgotten how to show a lady a good time."

Darryl Hannah as Pris in *Blade Runner*

Marion sticks with Indy, hoping to get the money he promised her for the medallion. She's kidnapped in a market, tied to a pole, seduced by the evil Belloq (Paul Freeman) (who doesn't get far when she drunkenly pulls a knife on him), gets thrown into a snake-infested pit and kidnapped again from a ship she and Indy are using to try to get the Lost Ark to safety. The women taking Marion's place in the following two sequels couldn't hold a candle to Allen.

Blade Runner (1982), Ridley Scott's stylish sci-fi noir, featured three women... Sean Young as Rachael, the beautiful replicant Deckard (Harrison Ford) falls for, and two of the nastiest female villains this side of the Milky Way, Pris and Zhora.

A group of escaped replicants have returned to Earth hoping to find their creator and prolong their short life span. Deckard is hot on their trail. Zhora (Joanna Cassidy)—"off world kick murder squad, talk about beauty and the beast, she's both"—is working in a dumpy club as an exotic dancer. Deckard, pretending to be a nerdy government official, questions her only to be elbowed in the stomach, punched in the face and strangled with his own necktie. Zhora is interrupted before she can finish off the gasping detective and flees through the rain-drenched streets. Deckard chases her firing; she is shot and crashes through a series of plate glass windows.

Pris (Darryl Hannah)—"a basic pleasure model, a standard item for military clubs in the outer colonies"—poses as a life-size doll when Deckard investigates the apartment where she is hiding. As he pulls a veil from her head, she kicks him before doing a series of flips that would make a gymnast envious and lands on his shoulders, her legs crushing his head between her thighs. She viciously smashes his face between her hands before backing up for another series of flips. Deckard shoots her. Like any typical noir, *Blade Runner*'s characters are neither totally good nor totally evil. Pris and Zhora die horrible deaths for merely wanting to live, although they might have gone about it in a kinder, gentler way.

1984 was a banner year for sci-fi fanatics. *Dune* debuted to less than raves, but Lady Jessica (Francesca Annis) was a worthy character going to great lengths to protect her son Paul (Kyle MacLachlan) from the evil Harkonnens, even jeopardizing the life of her unborn daughter.

2010, the sequel to *2001,* didn't inspire the awe and wonder the original did, but it did have something the earlier film didn't—female crew members. In fact, Helen Mirren captained the Russian ship.

Night of the Comet is a quirky sci-fi comedy with two Valley Girl heroines (who just happen to have had an artillery-loving father who taught them the pleasures of automatic weapons) taking on the zombies the comet has created. What to do when your entire world has been destroyed: that's right, go shopping! The girls (Catherine Mary Stewart and Kelli Maroney) manage to avoid the flesh-eating zombies and a group of deranged scientists before settling down with nice guy Hector (Robert Beltran) and two kids they saved from the scientists' lab. As the film closes Samantha (Maroney) happily finds another available young man and they drive off into the sunset.

James Cameron and Gale Anne Hurd would strike gold again with a little film that took the country by storm and made a mega-star of Arnold Schwarzenegger, *The Terminator*.

Linda Hamilton in *Terminator 2*

Sarah Conner (Linda Hamilton) is your average American girl, small apartment, lousy job and an indestructible robot from the future out to murder her before she can become the mother of a rebel leader. Rebel soldier Kyle Reese (Michael Biehn) arrives from the future to protect Sarah, who is slow to believe his wild story.

"Do I look like the mother of the future? Am I tough, organized? I can't even balance my checkbook."

The unrelenting terminator chases Sarah and Kyle to a factory. Sarah and a severely injured Kyle break in; an explosion kills Kyle. Sarah manages to crush the indestructible cyborg in a press.

Later, a very pregnant Sarah (she and Kyle did find a little time together) drives into the mountains with a German shepherd, a gun, and the courage to face an unknown future.

Sarah, like Ripley, was an average Jane who through extraordinary circumstances became something of a superwoman, a thing everyone hopes they could do if faced with similar threats.

In *Terminator 2: Judgment Day* (1991), Sarah has turned into a hardcore commando, committed to a mental institution for her belief in the coming apocalypse. Her son John (Edward Furlong) is now a teenager who hooks up with Arnold Schwarzenegger, this time playing the good terminator.

Jeff Goldblum and Geena Davis in *The Fly*

"She'd shack up with anybody she could learn from so she could teach me to be this great military leader."

They rescue Sarah from the institute and she sets out to kill the man responsible for creating the computer that will destroy the world. Armed to the teeth she fires into the man's home but misses. Sarah bursts into the house, but cannot kill him in cold blood. Arnold and John arrive and they convince Dyson (Joe Morton) to help them destroy the project he is working on as well as the chip from the earlier terminator, which was destroyed in the first film. Throughout the entire film they have been fleeing a new terminator, the T-1000, an indestructible creature of liquid metal. Sarah and Morton manage to destroy the lab, Morton giving his life to save the world and the group escapes followed by the T-1000. He is eventually melted in the bubbling vat of molten metal at a steel mill.

Sarah is not only a mother figure protecting her son, but the future of humanity as well.

In the remake of *The Fly* (1986), a courageous heroine is born this time in the statuesque form of Geena Davis who, as the lover of the mutating Jeff Goldblum, embraces the suffering, oozing creature, perhaps one of the most tender and truly heroic moments ever filmed. True

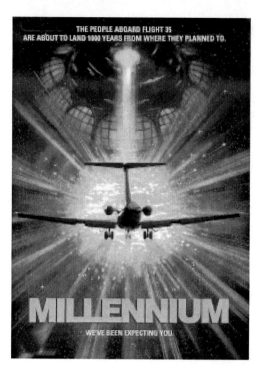

THE PEOPLE ABOARD FLIGHT 35 ARE ABOUT TO LAND 1000 YEARS FROM WHERE THEY PLANNED TO.

MILLENNIUM

WE'VE BEEN EXPECTING YOU

love really does conquer all. As in the original film she helps the pathetic creature she loves destroy himself.

Star Trek IV: The Voyage Home also debuted in 1986. *Star Trek* never had really strong female leads although Uhura was always along for the ride. However, Catherine Hicks as Dr. Gillian Taylor outwits the Enterprise crew by hitching a ride to the future to care for her beloved humpback whales.

Millennium (1989) has heroine-from-the-future Louise Baltimore (Cheryl Ladd) traveling into the past trying to stop time paradoxes from destroying the future. Louise leads teams to the past where they remove the victims of disasters before the event occurs. These people are taken to the future where they are society's last hope for saving the human race; the current inhabitants of the future are sterile, sickly creatures destroyed by harsh chemical pollution.

Science fiction as a genre has always been ahead of its time in its portrayal of characters and social conditions. *Millennium* is no exception. Based on a novel by John Varley, *Millennium* fell victim to bad casting and a confusing time travel story. However, Louise Baltimore was a strong female who was willing to go to any lengths to ensure the future of mankind.

The Abyss (1989) was a cursed project from day one. The shoot was way behind schedule and over budget because of the difficulty in filming in the huge underwater tank. Also, James Cameron and Gale Anne Hurd were quietly separating, a fact that didn't surface until after the film publicity tours were over. Whatever the problems, Mary Elizabeth Mastrantonio as Lindsey Brigman is exceptional. As the film opens, a military plane discharges its passengers. A sea of army boots descends followed by a pair of shapely legs in high heels.

"Oh no, look who's with them. Queen bitch of the universe."

Lindsay is not happy her project is being turned over to the "goon squad."

"Man, if Bud goes along with this, they're going to have to shoot her with a tranquilizer gun."

Bud Brigman, foreman of the underwater drilling rig Lindsey has designed, is contacted by the crew above and warned of an approaching hurricane, Fred.

"I don't know man. I think hurricanes should be named after women, don't you?" The tech laughs as papers begin to blow around and Lindsey, a walking hurricane, enters from outside. She speaks to Bud, miles below.

"Virgil, you wiener, you never could stand up to a fight."

Virgil, Bud's real name, comments to a shipmate, "God, I hate that bitch."

"Probably shouldn't have married her then, huh?"

A nuclear sub has been destroyed and rests on the edge of a deep abyss. A team of Navy Seals is sent down to the drilling rig to recover the warheads. Lindsey addresses the Seals on the dangers of the deep.

"We're been fully briefed, Mrs. Brigman."

"Just don't call me that. I hate that."

"All right. Well, what would you like us to call you, sir?"

Lindsey is the first to have contact with the aliens who reside in the abyss. Learning of the nuclear warhead the Seals have secretly taken aboard the rig, she pounds on their door with a fire extinguisher until they open the hatch. Lt. Coffey (Michael Biehn) is affected by the depth and is rapidly losing control. He climbs into a minisub trying to destroy

Ed Harris and Mary Elizabeth Mastrantonio in the powerful drowning scene from *The Abyss*.

the aliens, chased by Bud and Lindsey in another sub. Coffey damages their sub, which rapidly fills with water. The sub contains only one diving suit.

Bud: "You're smart, think of something."

Lindsey: "I've got a plan."

"What's the plan?"

"I drown and you tow me back to the rig."

Bud holds Lindsey close as she allows herself to drown in one frightening and touching scene. The sight of water beginning to fill the sub and Lindsey gasping for breath is chilling.

The crew manages to revive Lindsey and Bud decides to go over the edge of the abyss to retrieve the warhead. Lindsay keeps Bud focused as he dives further than any human being.

"It's not easy being a cast iron bitch. It takes discipline and years of training. A lot of people don't appreciate that."

Bud grins. The aliens save him and halt their attack on humanity because of the love between Bud and Lindsey. They still have some hope for the human race.

Michelle Pfeiffer as Catwoman in *Batman Returns*

Now we come to everyone's favorite anti-heroine, Michelle Pfeiffer, feline, feisty and ferocious as Catwoman in *Batman Returns* (1992). In a grotesque version of *Cinderella*, Selina Kyle is the mousy secretary to bad guy Max Shreck (Christopher Walken). At a business meeting Selina timidly speaks up, "I have a suggestion—well, actually, really more like a question."

"We haven't properly housebroken Miss Kyle, I'm afraid. In the plus column though, she makes a hell of a cup of coffee." Walken is bad to the bone and plays his evil part for all it's worth. Pfeiffer is outstanding as the confused Selina and vindictive Catwoman; she is one mean feline.

When the Penguin attacks, Selina is grabbed by a clown. Batman (Michael Keaton) comes to her rescue, Selina gives the clown a kick for good measure.

Danny DeVito and Michelle Pfeiffer in *Batman Returns*

"Wow. The Batman. Or is it just Batman? Your choice of course."

Batman stalks silently away.

"Well, that was very brief, just like all the men in my life. What men?" She looks at the fallen clown. "Then again there's you, but you need therapy."

Selina soon discovers the evil Shreck is up to no good.

"...Go ahead, intimidate me, bully me if it makes you feel big. I mean it's not like you can just kill me."

"Actually, it's a lot like that."

Shreck pushes Selina out a window, her broken body falls into the snow. Cats surround her and her eyes pop open. Stumbling home to her lonely apartment, she automatically listens to the messages on her answering machine—one sends her over the brink she has been tottering on.

"Hello, Selina Kyle. We're just calling to make sure you try Gotham Lady perfume. One whiff of this at the office and your boss will be asking you to stay after work for a candlelight staff meeting for two."

Selina trashes her apartment, smashes her pink neon sign that read "HELLO THERE" to now read "HELL HERE." She grabs a black leather coat from the closet, opens her sewing machine and emerges as Catwoman.

As a goon attacks a woman in an alley a shadow looms.

"I just love a big strong man who's not afraid to show it with someone half his size."

The goon approaches her menacingly. Catwoman, legs apart, exudes confidence, power and sensuality.

"Be gentle, it's my first time."

She kicks him four times before those deadly claws pop out. Catwoman hisses and slashes his face—tic-tac-toe—before the claws find his eyes.

The girl smiles "...thanks..." Catwoman grabs her face. "You make it so easy, don't you? Always waiting for some Batman to save you. I am Catwoman, hear me roar!"

The next day, Selina shows up at the office, very much alive—to Shreck's surprise—"Who'd have thought she had a brain to damage? She tries to blackmail me, I'll drop her out a higher window."

Catwoman breaks into Shreck's department store—happily playing with her new cat toy—a bullwhip. She skips rope and snaps the heads of mannequins before two guards spot her.

"I don't know whether to open fire or fall in love."

"You poor guys, always confusing your pistols with your privates."

"Don't hurt us lady, our take home's less than $300."

Catwoman places explosive devices in the store. Batman climbs after her to a roof where he tries to avoid hitting her, but finally has no other choice.

"How could you, I'm a woman!"

He approaches, "I'm sorry. I..." She kicks him in the stomach, and using her whip forces him over the side of the building.

Batman and Catwoman practice a bizarre courting ritual much like two little kids on a playground punching each other in the arm. However, their playground is the rooftops over Gotham City and they never stop punching each other. Catwoman slashes Batman's side while he napalms her arm. These two make an S&M practitioner seem normal.

Meanwhile, Selina and Bruce Wayne are engaging in their own courtship ritual. "It's the so-called normal guys who always let you down. Sickos never scare me—at least they're committed."

Later Catwoman sits on the chest of a stunned Batman, who had been gunned down by the police.

"You're catnip to a girl like me—handsome, dazed and to die for."

Catwoman finally corners Shreck in the underground hideout of the Penguin. Batman/Bruce tries to convince her to go away with him, "Let's just take him to the police then we can go home together."

"Bruce, I would love to live with you in your castle forever just like in a fairy tale." She slashes him, "I just couldn't live with myself, so don't pretend this is a happy ending."

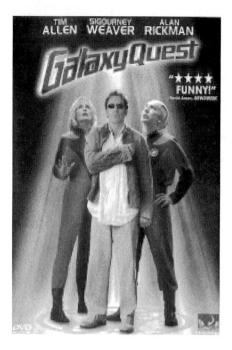

Shreck taking all this in can only think of one thing. "Selina Kyle, you're fired." He shoots Batman and then fires at Selina, but like all cats, she has nine lives and uses the last one to electrocute Shreck.

Bruce Wayne rides through the lonely snow covered streets of Gotham. Is that a shadow or a sequel?

The late 1990s offered a slew of gutsy women taking on the cinematic universe. The charming Sandra Bullock took on blond baddie Dennis Rodman in the humorous action sci-fi film *Demolition Man*, which takes a sly look at a future where everyone is just so nice and every restaurant is called Taco Bell. But like the classic *Metropolis*, the haves are still above-ground and a band of diligent rebels live beneath the city.

Sigourney Weaver returns to sci-fi, not as the doomed Ripley, but as the busty sci-fi diva in *Galaxy Quest*, an endearing tribute to sci-fi nerds everywhere, while another Academy Award winner, Mira Sorvino, portrays a scientist who tackles BEMs in *Mimic*. Carrie-Anne Moss efficiently took on *The Matrix*, while glorious scream queen Jamie Lee Curtis packed a double punch in the fun spy-thriller *True Lies* with Arnold Schwarzenegger and once again met up with the Shape in *Halloween H2O*. Curtis and screwball comedy were a perfect match as she portrays a bored housewife, who, while looking to spice up her life winds up in perilous situations with her secret-agent husband—who she thinks is a dull paper pusher. Disney would intelligently cast Curtis in their new 2003 comedy *Freaky Friday*, which appears to be a solid hit and should put Curtis on the Hollywood comeback road. Robert Heinlein's *Starship Troopers* finally hit the silver screen, but unfortunately with a thud, or is that dud? Fanboy favorite Denise Richards brings on the insecticide to help save the day, while *Clueless* sweetheart Alicia Silverstone made an appearance as Bat Girl in *Batman and Robin* (which, while reviled by critics and fans alike, is my favorite of the *Batman* series and a delightful homage to Lugosi's Monogram classics). As camp, *Starship Toopers* is one great movie, again the incredible BEMs take center stage. Another 1990s camp classic was comic-based *Tank Girl* starring Lori Petty and Ice-T in a postapocolyptic sci-fi comedy with Kangaroo Men, bad guy Malcolm McDowell and Iggy Pop. Finally, we have ultimate bitch/heroine—doctor, scientist, skeptic and love interest of Agent Mulder—Dana Scully (Gillian Anderson) in *The X-Files*. She's tortured, infected with

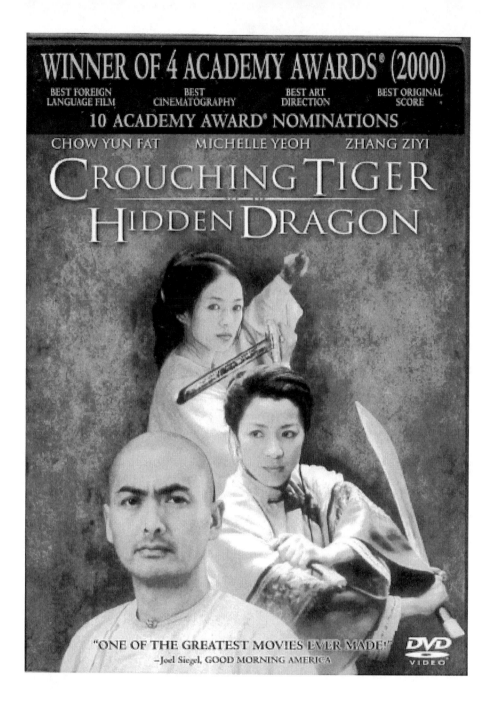

WINNER OF 4 ACADEMY AWARDS® (2000)

BEST FOREIGN LANGUAGE FILM   BEST CINEMATOGRAPHY   BEST ART DIRECTION   BEST ORIGINAL SCORE

10 ACADEMY AWARD® NOMINATIONS

CHOW YUN FAT   MICHELLE YEOH   ZHANG ZIYI

CROUCHING TIGER
HIDDEN DRAGON

"ONE OF THE GREATEST MOVIES EVER MADE!"
—Joel Siegel, GOOD MORNING AMERICA

DVD
VIDEO

cancer, impregnated with an alien baby, shot at, chased, terrorized and still manages to save the Earth from—well, we're still not sure what they saved the Earth from, but we know it was bad. And so the 1990s pass into history and we find women have gone from victims to outer space waitresses to real kick-ass heroes—and it only took about 80 years.

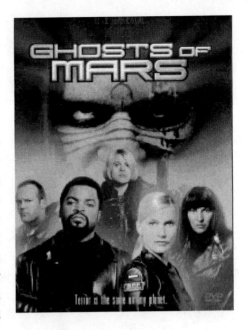

A new century has dawned—reality has taken over television, need we add reality bites? Ethics, morals and common decency have disappeared in the quest for ratings as anything, and we mean anything goes in TV land. On television we find: the Good—lots of roles for women; the Bad—TV husbands have turned into amiable morons incapable of any display of intelligence; and the Ugly—cruelty and morally bankrupt reality TV contestants. Sequels rule the box office, studios can't take any real chances you know. But fortunately, independent films are now critical darlings and even have their own awards show. The best movie of the summer of 2003 is a film based on a ride at Disneyland (*Pirates of the Caribbean*)! George Bush is in the White House, we're fighting in Iraq, the economy sucks, jobs keep disappearing—did we say 2003 or 1989? As we unhappily discovered in the 2000 election, those who don't learn from history are doomed to repeat it. But even if politics have reverted to the past, the women of today are producing movies, running film studios, earning mega bucks and creating their own roles. Virtually all sci-fi and horror films include multi-gender and multi-racial casts and women are no longer coffee-serving, fanboy eye candy. Even cartoons got into the act with female heroines from the Powerpuff Girls to the charming, belching, martial arts-fighting Princess Fiona (Cameron Diaz) in *Shrek*.

Ang Lee stunned audiences with his beautifully filmed and action-packed *Crouching Tiger, Hidden Dragon*, which featured not one, but two kick-ass heroines: Michelle Yeoh and Ziyi Zhang, mysterious beauties no man would dare cross. Drew Barrymore brought television's *Charlie's Angels* back to life with a powerhouse cast including Cameron Diaz and Lucy Liu, while Demi Moore, who returned from being a stay-

Natalie Portman as Queen Amidala in *Star Wars: The Phantom Menace*

at-home mom in a big way, made waves as the villain in the *Angels* sequel. Angelina Jolie brought a video game to vibrant life as wealthy, cunning and deadly archeologist/tomb raider Lady Lara Croft in two *Tomb Raider* films and Natalie Portman fought the Clone Wars as Queen and then Ambassador Amidala in *Star Wars* Episodes 1 and 2—although the special effects are state-of-the-art, the new series can't hold a candle to Princess Leia, Han Solo and Luke Skywalker. Little girls as well as big girls found feisty role models in genre films in the 2000s. Alexa Vega, as Carmen in *Spy Kids,* becomes a mini-James Bond as she takes on cartoonish villains. Meanwhile, little Emma Watson steals the show as the annoyingly intelligent and extraordinarily brave Hermione Granger in *Harry Potter and the Sorcerer's Stone* and *Harry Potter and the Chamber of Secrets.* Fantasy film fans are eagerly awaiting the return of Queen Amidala and Hermione in sequels scheduled for 2004 and 2005.

One can't really get too intellectually serious about any of these films; after all, *it's only a movie!* and nothing could be duller than long treatises on the feminine, social, anti-social, homosexual, violence, blah, blah, blah... effect of films. To me there is no better film than one that can

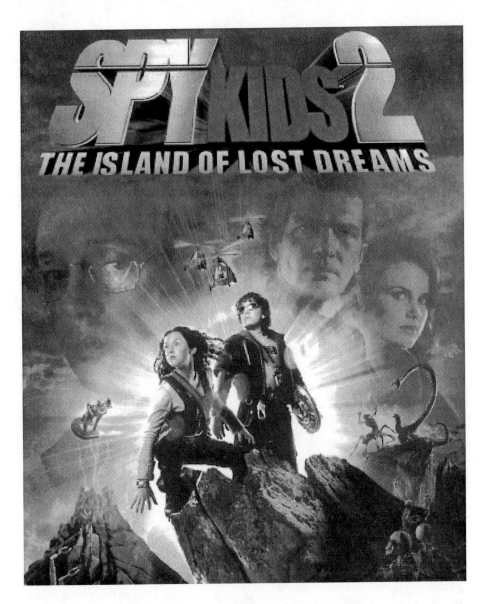

transport you to another time and another place, wiping away the harsh realities of life for a couple of hours. Like the man said, if you want to send a message, call Western Union.

I adore these female characters. They're fun, outrageous, daring and dynamic—wouldn't it be nice to have just a *little* of their chutzpah? Scream queens and hand-wringing maidens are rapidly fading into oblivion, but thankfully bitches will continue to reign supreme at the box office.

MAMIE VAN DOREN
Courtesy of Debbie Rochon

1960s bombshell Mamie Van Doren landed her first acting gig on a TV talk show at age 14. She worked on many films in bit parts until 1953 when she signed on with Universal and landed a featured role in *Forbidden*. In the 1950s she not only acted in dozens of films such as *High School Confidential*, *Untamed Youth* and *Teacher's Pet*, but also sang on rock and roll records.

In the '60s, Mamie made her indelible mark in film history by appearing in some now-cult classics including *Sex Kittens Go To College*, *The Private Lives Of Adam and Eve*, *Navy vs. The Night Monsters* and *Las Vegas Hillbillies*.

Were you just on a Mysteries and Scandals *show or something like that based on the Jayne Mansfield story?*

The Navy vs. the Night Monsters

Yes. First there was Marilyn; she opened the door for a lot of blondes. I knew Marilyn quite well. Jayne came from Texas after me. They both had tragic deaths, it was so sad. But I'm still hanging around.

Did it bother you being lumped together with these women?

Well I was always different. I was a rebel. I did a lot of teenage movies and was blacklisted from doing television. I did a lot of cult movies. I was blacklisted because I was big-busted.

Attack of the B Queens

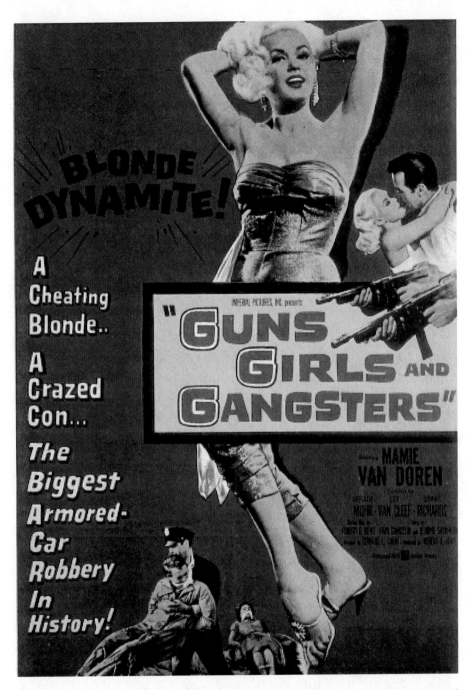

Did you ever find it a burden being used for your measurements?

Well I didn't know any different so it would be hard to tell. I wasn't happy with the roles I got. I was always a tough girl or a gangster's moll but I never got the guy you know!

I loved The Navy vs. the Night Monsters*!*

It was the yellow sweater! But I live on the beach now, work out a little, tan a little and live a very care-free life. I was at the Playboy Mansion on New Years Eve. I hit Hollywood quite often, and enjoy the big parties! I still swing when I get up there! I have fun wherever I go. Life is too short not to have fun.

What was it like touring Vietnam?

That changed my life forever! I got so many marvelous letters from the soldiers, I feel like I am really part of that war. I sang and entertained them; I tried to make them feel at home a little bit. And boy, they remember it well! I posted some of their letters. I went over there on my own and went to places no one else went! I went to places that Bob Hope didn't have the balls to go to.

What inspired you to go?

Jayne had gotten killed in 1967. I couldn't get a job at that point. I was an embarrassment and a reminder of the blondes of that time. So the war was escalating. We lost so many men. My agent suggested I go over there and entertain. I went in 1968, a time when we had so many wounded and spent so much of my time in hospitals. When the war was getting a little better I went back in 1971, I got very ill with dysentery so they had to air lift me out of there. I was in the hospital and almost died. When I got home and got better my life was never the same. I appreciated being alive every day after that. I had never been sick a day in my life before that. And seeing all the boys so hurt, it broke my heart. Only a person who has been there and has seen it, the smell of death, really knows what it's like. When I meet women who only want to talk about recipe books, I just can't relate, my life changed forever after being there.

Attack of the B Queens

STELLA STEVENS
Courtesy of Debbie Rochon

With over 100 film credits, Stella Stevens is one of the sexiest women in Hollywood. With her first cameo role in *Say One For Me* (1959) to her 1960 spread in the January edition of *Playboy* magazine, Stella was every man's fantasy in the '60s and '70s. While she looked exceptionally well and excelled in comedy, Ms. Stevens could also do drama. Her performances in serious roles in films such as *Too Late Blues* (1961) and *The Poseidon Adventure* (1972) proved her mettle as a dramatic actress. Perhaps her greatest asset is her longevity. Playing a plethora of parts, ranging from comedic cameos to heartfelt heroines, Stella has stuck around the acting game for five decades. She is a charming, personable and a hard-working lady. I feel very privileged to have had the opportunity to speak with her.

I understand you were discovered in the play?

Yes, I was discovered in the play *Bus Stop.* I got my first job in a department store in Memphis called Goldsmith's where I was making $38.36 a week. But I was proud to be working. Then a press agent from United Artists came through town and he told me if I could get to New York City while he was there he would introduce me to the executives of Twentieth Century Fox. So low and behold I took off for one week, went to

Stella Stevens and Jerry Lewis in *The Nutty Professor*

New York, and I did in fact meet the executives from Twentieth Century Fox. They wanted me to go out to Hollywood to test for a contract and maybe be the girl to play Jean Harlow in a forthcoming picture that Jerry Wald was going to shoot.

It was like a dream. It was really fast. But I did come out to California and I wrote my own screen test scene from a Harold Robbins novel called *79 Park Avenue*. It actually had a line in it that read "What's a nice girl like you doing in a business like this?" and I answered that question by wearing a skimpy black corset and a garter belt and hose! So I got the contract!

What was your first movie?

My very first film was called *Say One For Me* with Bing Crosby and Bob Wagner and Debbie Reynolds. I played a chorus girl dancing directly behind Debbie Reynolds who was the lead singer/dancer in the scene. It was a really fun film with my really good friend, my first director and my mentor Frank Tashlin. He had done lots and lots of films that were comedies and worked a lot with Dean Martin and Jerry Lewis. So when I went to Paramount Pictures, Frank introduced me to Jerry Lewis which led to Jerry putting me in *The Nutty Professor*, which is still a classic.

The appeal you brought to that movie was the combination of such beauty and great comedic abilities.

I experienced a strange thing, some reviewer had said when the movie was first released back in '63, that I looked too old to be a college student! I thought wait a minute, I'm wearing puppy dog ears, and I know I am the right age, I actually would be in college if I wasn't making the film. Then I saw the movie again last year, a friend of mine played it for me in his home theater, and it was the first time I had seen it in over 30 years. I watched my performance and I said, "It's not that I looked old, I just act mature." My actions and the way I held myself were mature, it's not that I looked too old for the part at all. I hope I don't look too old now!

You also worked with Bobby Darin, another top sex symbol back then.

I loved Bobby Darin; we had such a great time together in the movie, we made *Too Late Blues* together, which is still one of my favorite movies, of course directed by John Cassvetes; a wonderful actor and a good friend. We had a tribute screening of *The Poseidon Adventure* over the millennium New Years and someone asked me who was the best kisser, the most romantic of all. I answered saying, well how can I put this delicately, Bobby Darin kissed me once and got an enormous erection. I cannot get that out of my mind, every time I think of Bobby Darin I think of that. He was for real, I mean when he kissed

you onscreen he felt it for real! I think that was the sexiest onscreen kiss I have ever had.

Did you ever get tired of being so beautiful, did it ever stand in your way career-wise?

Obviously you have not seen my movie *The Granny!* In that movie I play an 86-year-old woman. It's a black comedy. In the movie I get a magic potion to drink which cannot be left out in the sun. Well my granddaughter leaves it out in the sun of course and after drinking the potion it kills me. Then I awaken in the morgue alive after death and I'm Super-empowered and I kill my entire family in the most grotesque manner. It's very funny actually! I was certainly not young and beautiful in that film! I was not allowed to look pretty whatsoever in that one. I have done so many different movies and have tried to always look a little different. I can always see through my own characterization and see me behind it, but I'm hoping the good facade will fool people in the characters!

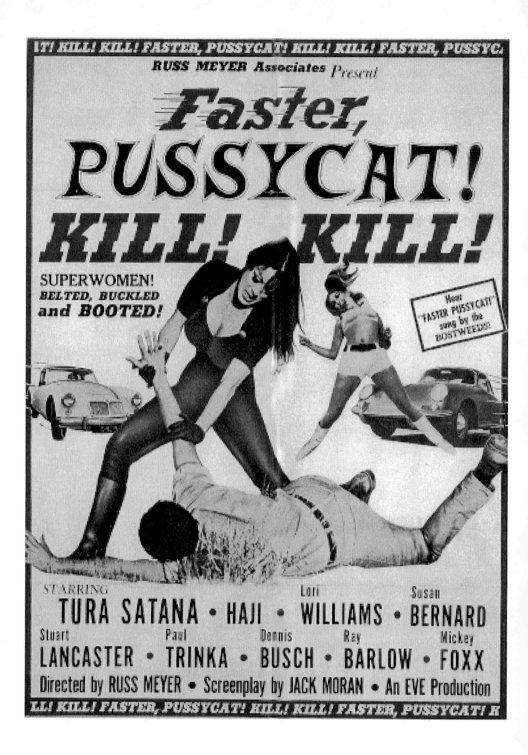

TURA SATANA: *FASTER PUSSYCAT, KILL! KILL!* In Her Own Words

Shortly after my first marriage didn't work out, I started out as a singer and legitimate dancer in some of the clubs in Chicago, then I went to Hollywood to see if I could do any better there. But out there I was one of many lovely young ladies all trying for the same thing. Only I wouldn't do it via the casting couch. So, I did some nude modeling for Harold Lloyd, the silent comedian. He fell in love with my face and figure. He was the one person who really kept me trying to put my foot in the door, because he told me that if just one producer or director ever got to see me in front of a camera, then that would be all she wrote. So, I kept trying. Unfortunately, for me, I got make-up poisoning from some bad make-up that I used and it broke my face out so badly that I lost my job as a waitress. It was a very severe case of make-up poisoning. I finally headed back to Chicago, because I couldn't work and support myself for a time.

Once there and with my face cleared up, it was easy to get a job as a dancer. I got a job in Calumet City, Illinois at the Rendezvous Club. Once there, the boss said that I had too good a figure to keep it covered and he offered me $75.00 a week more if I would strip. There was an act coming in that would need a dancer for their show. So, I got the job and began my strip career as Galatea, the statue that comes to life. It was a very interesting concept and the audiences loved it and my dancing. I finally got tired of doing that and decided to go it on my own as a dancer. I knew that with my martial arts background that I would be able to do a lot of acrobatics in my routine that none of the other gals could do. From Calumet City, I went to New Orleans and worked there for approximately 2 years. I developed quite the following there, even though there was a lot of prejudice against Japanese, but not as much as there was against the Negroes. Until I signed with my agent Mike Riaff, I wasn't really making any money, but

after I signed with him, it was a matter of weeks and then all of a sudden I was making more money and getting headliner billing. From clubs I went into the burlesque theaters and learned a whole new set of moral codes. I know that most people think that strippers are either whores or tramps back then, but that was definitely not the case. In burlesque, you never tried to steal someone else's boyfriend by walking around with nothing on. As soon as you came offstage, the wardrobe mistress was standing there with your robe. No nudity was allowed backstage. I learned quite a bit from a lady by the name of Stunning Smith, the lady with the purple hair. She taught me to use the stage and not to waste it. She also taught me to really work my audiences. I really thank her for all of her help and kindness to a newcomer and greenhorn. She was one of the nicest ladies I ever worked with on the burlesque circuit.

During the 18 years that I worked in the burlesque theaters and nightclubs, I got to meet some of the finest and most talented dancers of any era. Among them were Lili St. Cyr; Tempest Storm; Maxine Martin; the skyscraper girl, Stunning Smith; Sally Rand; Rose La Rose; Candy Barr; Blaze Starr; Ming Lee; China Lee; Suzanne Summers and a multitude of others. I think that one of the highlights of my life was when Eddie Foy came onstage my first time in the Grand Theater in St. Louis and presented me with two dozen long stem roses. He told me that he had never enjoyed a dancer so much as he had enjoyed my performance. The sec-

Attack of the B Queens

ond highlight was when Elvis did the very same thing at the Follies Theater in Chicago. The third time was when I was voted one of the TEN BEST UNDRESSED of the world. I was in some very classy company then.

It was while I was working at the Follies Theater in downtown LA, that a director from Warner Bros. came into see my show, because he had heard about an Oriental female dancer who was built quite well. That was when I got my first job in a TV series, *The Hawaiian Eye*. Once the camera got ahold of me, it seemed that I was constantly getting calls for interviews for this series or that series, but never without being propositioned, so I didn't get a lot of parts when I said "No."

When I was working in the Pink Pussycat Club on Santa Monica Blvd., Billy Wilder and I.A.L. Diamond came in there with their wives. When I came out on stage both Billy and his wife said that I was the Suzette Wong that he needed for his film *Irma La Douce*. While working on that film, I got the call for *Faster Pussycat, Kill! Kill!* Needless to say, when Russ Meyer told me to just make Varla come alive, I did that. After that, then I did *Astro Zombies*, *The Doll Squad* and *Who's Been Sleeping in My Bed*, plus several TV series in between. It was like Harold Lloyd said, once the camera caught me, we had a love affair. The camera was always kind to me and I thank God for the gift of beauty and talent that He gave me to use.

I remember one time during the filming of *Faster Pussycat, Kill! Kill!* that Russ and I were having a difference of opinion on how a scene should be done. I got so angry that I turned around and punched a railroad tie wall. I wound up bruising my hand quite a bit, thank goodness I was wearing gloves at the time, but after that, Russ said that if I felt that strongly about the scene then we would do it my way. It turned out well, because it was the scene where the Porsche and the Vegetable go at it. I will say that working with Russ is definitely a learning process.

The only thing that was wrong was that *Faster Pussycat, Kill! Kill!* was ahead of its time. But, everyone caught up eventually. My advice to any females who are set on getting in films is that they don't give up trying and don't sell themselves short. Just know that you can do it and do it well.

BARBARA LEIGH:
VAMPIRELLA
In Her Own Words

I moved to Los Angeles from Tennessee in 1967 when I was 19 with my husband and son Gerry, and shortly afterwards we separated. I remained in LA, and he went back to Tennessee.

I worked as a doctor's assistant at the time, and was invited to go into Beverly Hills with a couple of the nurses to a nightclub called The Other Place. When we were in the audience the performer that night, Mark Devlon, spotted me in the crowd and later came to our table to say hello and introduce himself. Mark was incredibly handsome, and asked if he could call me. Of course,

the other nurses were jealous, but I was flattered and I gave him my number. He called me later that night, and shortly afterward [we] became engaged.

Mark let it be known that I was wasting my time working as a nurse, and thought I was bound for a successful modeling and acting career. Mark arranged to have a photographer friend of his take pictures of me, which were later sold to Kodak. The pictures led to a modeling contract and gave birth to my career. Mark and I ultimately didn't get married and we split one week before the wedding. He wasn't ready for children, but one door closed and another opened.

Soon after our split I was sitting outside a restaurant called Mirabelles when celebrity hairstylist Gene Shacove spotted me and asked me to do a hair commercial for Clairol. Gene was the inspiration behind the movie *Shampoo*, starring Warren Beatty. Dating Gene had its perks because he owned a famous nightclub also in Beverly Hills called The Candy Store, and once again I was discovered at a nightclub.

An agent came to my table and asked if I'd ever thought about acting. I said yes. He gave me his card and asked me to call to setup an appointment. The agency was then called IFA, which is now the world-famous ICM. I made the appointment, and when I arrived several days later Allan Rappaport met me with Dick Clayton who was a big agent at that time and had discovered James Dean. Dick also had a very impressive celebrity clientele including Jane Fonda and Burt Reynolds, who was emerging as a budding superstar. We hit it off and he signed me on the spot. I also went with IFA for commercials and soon got my first national commercial for Coke where I played a girl in a harem being traded on the Sahara desert for a Coke. I got to ride a camel, which was fun.

At that time my name was Barbara Haynes but the screen actors guild already had a Barbara Haynes so I had to change my name. Randy Fred who was my agent was reading the paper one day when he said "Vivian Leigh has died." Someone else yelled out, "That's it—Barbara Leigh," which is how I got my name.

I retired from the business after only 10 years due to my project with *Vampirella*, a comic strip character with a huge cult following. I was under contract to Hammer Films in England to star in the movie version of *Vampirella* and was signed to a five-picture deal. Unfortunately, the film was never made but Warren Comics went on to put my pictures as *Vampirella* on eight of its covers, immortalizing me forever as a part of her history.

Barbara's book, *The King, McQueen and the Love Machine* is available at www.Xlibris.com. She can also be visited at www.barbaraleigh.com.

AMY LYNN BEST
Courtesy of Seth Roman

Amy Lynn Best is a rising star in the world of independent film. Making her acting and producing debut with the short film *Tenants*, she moved on to produce and co-star in the feature *The Resurrection Game* as the leather-clad zombie exterminator Sister Mary Bliss, along with cameo roles in Ryan Cavaline's *Day of the Axe 3* and Paul Scrabo's outrageous comedy *Dr. Horror's Erotic House of Idiots.*

On her role in Resurrection Game*:*

Sister Bliss is a dominatrix/marriage counseling/zombie-killing nun! Since Sister Bliss was written for me, my little oddities and idiosyncrasies, I'm basically playing myself, but up a couple of notches. The dialogue between myself and Bill [Homan, the film's co-producer who plays rival exterminator Simon MacForman] sound a lot like us in real life. We enjoy joking and kidding and insulting each other. All we had to do was to broaden the banter. She's a very strong woman, she's very determined. She knows what she wants to do and what she has to do, but she still seems like she has something to prove. There she is, doing a lot of things that people don't approve of. Not just the dominatrix thing, but the exterminations—there are so many people in that world who don't approve the private exterminator thing and would rather leave it up to a firm called NOE. And her history was more or less in the script—writer/director Mike Watt's scripts are always detailed—so I didn't have to create a backstory so much as "this is who she is." I did sit down and think about how she would feel in each situation. Is she going to be mad, scared, happy, what? And the fact that I'm doing so many things on the set, I'm thankful that she is so close to me, only exaggerated, that it doesn't take a lot of preparation.

On strong heroines in movies and television:

It's definitely the feminist in me saying the women are in charge, so shut up and listen to us, because we're the only ones who can help around here. There are not a lot of movies, let alone low-budget movies, that have the women in charge—though lately I have been seeing a lot more. Like *Buffy the Vampire Slayer* and [Pat Bishow's independent video] *The Girls from H.A.R.M.*, where the women are going around kicking butt. In *The Resurrection Game*, it's not necessarily kicking butt, but the women are definitely smarter. They have a better handle on what's going on and get it, rather than just reacting to what's around them—which is what people criticize women for in general. I don't like it when a woman who's proven herself to be a Tae Kwan Do expert suddenly gets into danger and starts screaming and biting her nails, just because the guy has to come in and rescue her.

GAIL HARRIS
Courtesy of *GC Magazine*

Gail Harris shares about her experience starring in director Jim Wynowski's *The Haunting of Morella* in which she plays an English serving maid. Though her first exposure to the horror genre, Gail speaks with zest about the experience. "Among my scenes they buried me in a hole in the ground. First they covered me in death make-up with lumps of flesh hanging off and they used this make-up that would attract flies. Then they dug a hole in the ground in the forest and they laid me in the hole and they covered me in leaves. My hands were left sticking out like a dead body. The characters have to brush away the leaves and I have to lie there with my eyes open, unblinking, while all this dirt is falling in my face and flies are landing on my face. At one point Jim says, 'We can see your pulse moving. Can you stop that?' "

GINGER LYNN ALLEN
Courtesy of Rick Ryan
GC Magazine

In 1984, Ginger Lynn hit the world of adult film like a storm. But in the late '80s she abandoned that world and sought a career in mainstream acting.

How did that first B movie role come about?
One of the reasons I stopped doing adult films was because I wanted more. I wanted to do more and act more—I was so into the acting. I mean, I love sex but I wanted bigger roles and more of a challenge. So I studied acting for several years and I tried to find an agent. Initially, it was difficult to get an agent so I went and bought all of the Hollywood magazines that let you know what films are in production. I had head-shots made up. I made up a resume using real titles from my films but used the ones that didn't sound like they came from a porno film. And I sent them out and went on this audition for the film *Wild Man*. And I went in for my first audition and went through three callbacks, and on the third callback the director was there—and of all people it was Freddy Lincoln, a director who had directed adult film. I walked in and I was like, "Freddy, what are you doing here?" And he said he was directing the film and he had no idea I was one of the people coming in. And he said I was the best person for the role.

That's curious, because I know that back in the late '60s and '70s there were a lot of porn directors who were doing mainstream films under assumed names.
That's still true. Because of loyalty I cannot say who or what, but there is one major television sitcom that has been on for years and the director is someone who came from adult films and still produces and directs adult films under another name.

Your B film Cleo/Leo *has become something of a cult hit. How do you feel about that?*

I love *Cleo/Leo*! It's one of my all-time favorite B movies that I've made and, ironically, the woman who directed and produced my most recent adult movie—after a 13-year retirement—is Veronica Hart, who is also Jamie Hamilton, who is the lead in *Cleo/Leo*. It was such a fun film to make. I got to play such a bubbly, ditsy, dingy, fun character and, believe it or not, people believe that women who do bimbos have it easy. It's hard to be a bimbo unless you really are one! And if you really are one you usually can't act.

Was there any difficulty doing horror movies after having done porn?

I've only done a couple of horror films. I did *Buried Alive*. I did a film called *Satan's Storybook*, and then I did a film that hasn't been released called *Lost Souls*. And, for some reason, I don't get cast very often in horror films. I don't know if I look too nice, or what their problem is. I enjoy them and I had fun. It wasn't very difficult, it was just very different. And, I'm not good at screaming unless I'm having an orgasm. (Laughter)

What are some of your favorite B film roles and why?

I don't know if *Bound and Gagged: A Love Story* is considered a B film. It's definitely an independent film. It's not in the mainstream genre as a big-budget film, so I guess you would classify that as B. But, *Bound and Gagged* would definitely be my absolute all-time favorite B movie. The character that I play is a girl who has had a lot of religious things shoved down her throat. She marries a man who's very abusive and I'm somewhat schizophrenic. And the director and producers gave me such a wonderful character to play with who had so many different levels. I was able to show off some of my talents.

JACKIE LOVELL
Courtesy of *GC Magazine*

It was the feature movie *Femalien* that gave Jackie Lovell her break: "*Femalien* was really the first film where I had a big role. I was supporting the lead. They wanted me so badly—they begged me for three months to be the alien and I said no because at that time, I'm like, this is my first big role with dialogue and there is no way I'm going to be able to figure out how to connect with the thoughts of an alien. I wanted it to be real and it wouldn't have been real. Being the alien—the connection wasn't there and I knew I was going to be so nervous cause this was my first big thing and I was like, 'I just want to be the hippie girl' cause I can relate and it'll be natural and not so nerve-racking."

Working on *Femalien* drew the attention of Full Moon Pictures who saw Lovell on the set and liked her. They called her and asked for her to take the lead in *Head of the Family*: "I've loved horror movies my whole life and I thought it was so cool that I was getting to be in horror movies. I got the lead (in *Head of the Family*) and I thought if I never get another movie again I want to do the best job I can. So I did everything I had learned from acting classes and it ended up turning out really nice. After that, people just started calling me for different movies."

KATHY KURTZ
Courtesy of
Kevin Lindenmuth

Kathy Kurtz gives her advice to aspiring actors:

Think really hard before you give your life to it. First, take into account that if you really love it…well…sometimes it sucks to make your hobby your job. You have to have a will of steel to pursue acting as a profession. For every available role there are at least 100 actors trying to get it. And your initial investment is a major one. Head shots, professional resumes, composites and audition clothes don't come cheap. Count on lots of various day jobs, because if you do get a role, you need your boss to be flexible. And remember that you're going to live your life never knowing where your next job is coming from.

Auditions can be grueling and very debasing. Countless hours of waiting around with three pages of script in your hand, pacing endlessly, only to be seen by a table full of guys who have been in the same room for hours saying "Relax, be yourself." Then they just stare and stare at you while you do silly things and try to make them seem natural. Who gets the part? The phoniest people they can find.

Or agents will tell you "It's for the part of the secretary so dress the part" and you go out and find the best looking business suit you can find, even though it's $100 and you don't have a job and show up there to find that they've given the part to the girl in the bikini top. I guess they didn't say what kind of secretary she was…

Or they read you and read you for three hours until you're the last one left there, called back three times to read even more, given the script and told to learn the lines, only to find out one week before rehearsals began that they cast someone else, who just happened to be sleeping with the director! I'm really not making this up, all these things have really happened to me.

What I'm trying to say is that a performing life is very difficult, so you really have to love what you're doing and have the resolve to wade through all the bullshit and still enjoy what you're doing. And if you're lucky, you get involved on a good project with decent pay, like the one I'm involved with now. And when the applause comes, well, it's just like great sex. So you need to keep at it, you need courage, and need self-confidence, you need determination and not just a little bit of insanity helps, too.

LESLIE CULTON
Courtesy of
Kevin Lindenmuth

Worst acting experiences: "In *Terror at Tate Mansion*, my death scene required me to spend 2 hours in a freezing shower and 4 hours in (fake) blood-soaked panties. Your private parts are not meant to be in stage blood that long! Also it was a Georgia summer and the air conditioning is cranked up and I am naked, bloody and freezing! The crew goes off to get in a real short pick-up shot and forgets me! I sit and wait and wait and wait, Jenny Wallace came in and saved me from hypothermia. In *April's Fool* where I was a dancer, it was supposed to be a very seedy bar and they told me that although they loved me, I was too attractive to be realistic in their dive strip club!"

PATRICIA TALLMAN
Courtesy of Mike Watt

Patricia Tallman is best known to horror fans as the revisionist Barbara in Tom Savini's 1990 remake of *Night of the Living Dead*. To science fiction fans, she was the telepathic Lyta on *Babylon 5*. She's also an accomplished stage actress and stuntperson, having doubled for Gates McFadden on *Star Trek: The Next Generation* and Laura Dern in *Jurassic Park*. She's an actress who loves her craft and while she takes every job seriously, she tries to find the fun in every role.

What was your reaction to the character of Barbara in the script to the remake of Night of the Living Dead?

I was pleasantly surprised. When I first heard they were remaking *Night of the Living Dead*, I could not imagine why. It was so scary in black and white and so raw in the way it was shot. But then I read the script and thought, "Oh this is so much better." I don't think I would have done it had it been exactly the same. I didn't want to be a screaming female. But George wrote her with a whole new twist, gave her a spine, and that was a lot of fun to do. He wrote her like that and then I just got to fill in between the black of the page. He put in the black and I put in the white. I like the fact that Barbara was this little school teacher person. A normal little lady who was probably very unused to standing up for herself at all until this happened. I like that I got the chance to make that transformation, where she goes from being a normal person. And maybe the fans could get the feeling that that could be anybody— that could be them! You never know how brave you can be. You may not think you're a brave person, but if you're pushed up against the wall, you would do what you could! And everyone likes to think they would, right? So that was a pleasure in being her. She didn't start off being Red Sonja. She was a normal lady in an extraordinary circumstance.

SASHA GRAHAM
Courtesy of Kevin Lindemuth

Sasha Graham has appeared in 15 horror films from 1995 to 2002 including *Addicted to Murder* (1995), *Psycho Sisters* (1996) and *Rage of the Werewolf* (1999). Here, Sasha shares some thoughts on acting and her experiences.

Do you consider yourself a Scream Queen?

Well, I don't see myself as a Scream Queen. Yes, I've done some horror films. I've also been in over 15 plays produced here in New York City, worked on soaps, on Comedy Central, done interactive dinner theater, and was the spokesgirl for an anti-smoking educational CD-ROM. I'm an actress. I don't want to be labeled as anything except as someone who does good work.

What is the weirdest experience you've had on a feature?

I've had a few. I would say eating in the restaurants in Akron, Ohio while shooting Bookwalter's *Polymorph* and my cameo in *Bloodletting*. They actually have potato chips listed as an appetizer on the menus out there. Weird! What can I say, I'm a spoiled New Yorker. Also, holding a handful of mealworms for *Alien Agenda: Out of the Darkness* was weird and disgusting, an experience I do not wish to repeat. As for *Vicious Sweet*—I felt like the character was written just like me. Except for the fact that, thank God, I've never been abducted.

What are your favorite horror movies?

Oh, where do I start? I love movies so much!!! I love old-fashioned slasher flicks like *Friday the 13th* and *Halloween*. They still scare me to death. I'm a huge fan of David Lynch as well. The big-budget alien movies are a lot of fun, too. *Alien, Close Encounters, E.T., First Contact, Independence Day* and, of course, the end all to be all of all sci-fi movies, *Star Wars*. I think it's because they're more fantasy than reality—you can pretty much assure yourself that what happens in the movie won't ever happen to you. I'd rather find myself on an alien vessel than be trapped in Jeffrey Dahmer's basement!

You've gotten your start in movies through low-budget productions. Do you see yourself working on them for a few more years?

Absolutely! Low-budget movies are great, in the fact that everyone is involved for the love of the film. Trust me, you can't get a crew member or actor to give up their weekend and spend 10 hours on a set for little or no pay if they don't absolutely love the fact that they are making a great movie. Look at *Clerks, Brothers McMullen* and *Welcome to the Dollhouse.* America is finally ready and willing to accept low-budget films. I think there is much more room to take chances, break the rules, and create a really fabulous film when you're doing an independent feature.

TINA KRAUSE
Courtesy of Mike Watt

Tina Krause, as the legend goes, was walking around a Chiller convention as a fan when she was approached by a producer to shoot a small scene for an upcoming WAVE movie. Twenty minutes and a death scene later, Tina had a new career option in front of her. Almost 10 years later, she's performed in over 50 movies, including Pete Jacalone's original *Psycho Sisters*, Zachary Winston Snygg's *In the Hood* and J.R. Bookwalter's character-driven in-name-only sequel *Witchouse 3: Demon Fire*. Recently, the actress has turned her attention to writing and producing her own films, including the award-winning short film, *Phone Tag* and the upcoming feature *Limbo*.

How was working on Witchouse 3?

Cool, very cool. I got to meet a lot of great new people out there. The way [Tempe Entertainment] runs things was different. It wasn't like the usual stuff that I do on the East Coast. It was more professional the way it was handled. Rose [my character] was cool to play. It wasn't a hard character to do because, basically, I don't know if [J.R. Bookwalter] had me in mind when he wrote it, but he wrote it to my personality. Which could have been a mistake. [laughs] So it was easy to do as far as the character goes. But she was fun to do.

What prompted your decision to get away from the low-budget T&A fetish stuff that dominated the early part of your career?

One day I was watching all the stuff I was doing, and I saw one scene in one that I liked–and I can't remember the movie, unfortunately–and the rest of the stuff you could just tell that I was bored, and just wasn't into it. And it hit me that, yeah, I don't really want to do this. And when I saw myself do something that I would actually call talented, I realized that I was never going to be taken seriously if I don't get out of this. I was going to have to change and make a mark in a lot of different ways. Not just in acting, but I'd have to make a mark in directing, in writing, understand how to actually act. I hate to say "understand how to act" because that makes it seem that I don't know what I'm doing. That's not what I mean. I mean that once you explore different areas there are so many different things–when people give you direction, you have to be able to see it from the other side, in order to actually be good at what you do. Writing and visualizing things, seeing things from the conceptual side, helped me to move on, I guess you could say. I love the acting and directing by far. But I just can't keep doing the monotonous roles that weren't challenging me. And they really weren't challenging me for a good long while. I'm getting away from it completely. I have to get away from it. I'm going on to other things now. Actually my fans have been very cool about my not wanting to do [the simulated snuff-horror that WAVE specializes in] any more. They've supported me on my decision.

Has the change been successful?

Yeah. Very much. Now I'm getting offered roles where I get to play a different nationality. It's going to be different. I don't know how the make-up is going to work, but I'm going to have to study, figure out how to do this character justice. But I do study. When I played a psychopath in *Day of the Axe 3*, I took my butt up to an institution. Just checked it out. Hung around for a day. I lied, told them I was a student studying psychology and came up with some silly little thing to cover. I sat there the whole day and took notes and studied. If that's my role, I'll do it.